AMERICA'S SECURITY ROLE IN THE SOUTH CHINA SEA

HEARING

BEFORE THE

SUBCOMMITTEE ON ASIA AND THE PACIFIC

OF THE

COMMITTEE ON FOREIGN AFFAIRS
HOUSE OF REPRESENTATIVES

ONE HUNDRED FOURTEENTH CONGRESS

FIRST SESSION

JULY 23, 2015

Serial No. 114–77

Printed for the use of the Committee on Foreign Affairs

Available via the World Wide Web: http://www.foreignaffairs.house.gov/ or
http://www.gpo.gov/fdsys/

U.S. GOVERNMENT PUBLISHING OFFICE

95–637PDF   WASHINGTON : 2015

For sale by the Superintendent of Documents, U.S. Government Publishing Office
Internet: bookstore.gpo.gov   Phone: toll free (866) 512–1800; DC area (202) 512–1800
Fax: (202) 512–2104   Mail: Stop IDCC, Washington, DC 20402–0001

COMMITTEE ON FOREIGN AFFAIRS

EDWARD R. ROYCE, California, *Chairman*

CHRISTOPHER H. SMITH, New Jersey
ILEANA ROS-LEHTINEN, Florida
DANA ROHRABACHER, California
STEVE CHABOT, Ohio
JOE WILSON, South Carolina
MICHAEL T. McCAUL, Texas
TED POE, Texas
MATT SALMON, Arizona
DARRELL E. ISSA, California
TOM MARINO, Pennsylvania
JEFF DUNCAN, South Carolina
MO BROOKS, Alabama
PAUL COOK, California
RANDY K. WEBER SR., Texas
SCOTT PERRY, Pennsylvania
RON DeSANTIS, Florida
MARK MEADOWS, North Carolina
TED S. YOHO, Florida
CURT CLAWSON, Florida
SCOTT DesJARLAIS, Tennessee
REID J. RIBBLE, Wisconsin
DAVID A. TROTT, Michigan
LEE M. ZELDIN, New York
DANIEL DONOVAN, New York

ELIOT L. ENGEL, New York
BRAD SHERMAN, California
GREGORY W. MEEKS, New York
ALBIO SIRES, New Jersey
GERALD E. CONNOLLY, Virginia
THEODORE E. DEUTCH, Florida
BRIAN HIGGINS, New York
KAREN BASS, California
WILLIAM KEATING, Massachusetts
DAVID CICILLINE, Rhode Island
ALAN GRAYSON, Florida
AMI BERA, California
ALAN S. LOWENTHAL, California
GRACE MENG, New York
LOIS FRANKEL, Florida
TULSI GABBARD, Hawaii
JOAQUIN CASTRO, Texas
ROBIN L. KELLY, Illinois
BRENDAN F. BOYLE, Pennsylvania

AMY PORTER, *Chief of Staff*   THOMAS SHEEHY, *Staff Director*
JASON STEINBAUM, *Democratic Staff Director*

———————

SUBCOMMITTEE ON ASIA AND THE PACIFIC

MATT SALMON, Arizona *Chairman*

DANA ROHRABACHER, California
STEVE CHABOT, Ohio
TOM MARINO, Pennsylvania
JEFF DUNCAN, South Carolina
MO BROOKS, Alabama
SCOTT PERRY, Pennsylvania
SCOTT DesJARLAIS, Tennessee

BRAD SHERMAN, California
AMI BERA, California
TULSI GABBARD, Hawaii
ALAN S. LOWENTHAL, California
GERALD E. CONNOLLY, Virginia
GRACE MENG, New York

CONTENTS

AMERICA'S SECURITY ROLE IN THE SOUTH CHINA SEA

THURSDAY, JULY 23, 2015

House of Representatives,
Subcommittee on Asia and the Pacific,
Committee on Foreign Affairs,
Washington, DC.

The subcommittee met, pursuant to notice, at 2 o'clock p.m., in room 2172 Rayburn House Office Building, Hon. Scott Perry [acting chairman of the subcommittee] presiding.

Mr. SHERMAN. Folks, we are about 25 minutes late, which is fine. The problem is that we have Secretary Kerry and Secretary Moniz briefing the Democrats on—I think there is something going on here that they are concerned about.

And so I am just going to deliver what would be my opening remarks. If the gavel hasn't fallen, then these are unofficial random statements that I made for your entertainment before the hearing could begin. This is certainly not our first hearing on the South China Sea.

We have got to take it seriously, and yet we shouldn't get carried away. And my fear is that we are making a mountain out a reef, just as not only China but I believe four other countries have already added dirt on top of these islets to make them bigger than God intended them to be.

We should remember there is no oil under these islets, and if there is it is not ours. And we should resist the tendency of the Pentagon to try to reconfigure itself as an entity devoted chiefly to fighting China in the South China Sea. I already see that in their research and increasingly in their procurement.

I think it is important that the Pentagon be focused on the conflict we do have, which is with worldwide Islamic extremist terrorism. Those who are—and there is a lot of reasons for people on all sides of this to hype its importance. One of the ways you hype the importance is you say that $5 trillion of trade goes through the South China Sea.

Well, the vast majority of that is going into Chinese ports or coming out of Chinese ports, which means that China is threatening to interdict its own trade—a threat they are not making and that I wouldn't be taking seriously if they did.

So, first, you have got to count how much trade is going into a Chinese port, then how much is coming out. Then you have got to be careful not to count trade coming out of a Japanese port as South China Sea or relevant ocean area transit, if it is going to a

Chinese port. And when you are done with that, you realize that the amount of trade we are talking about is still significant. And we still have an interest in demonstrating to China that we believe in freedom of navigation.

No one doubts America's right to the Hawaiian islands. It is undisputed. But the United States does not assert that we have a naval exclusion zone on one-third of the Pacific Ocean, namely that portion between San Francisco, or I should say Los Angeles, and Hawaii. So the Pentagon would like to see a worthy adversary.

Every time our military has faced an asymmetrical, non-uniformed enemy, it has been a terrible experience. Sometimes victorious, but always a terrible experience, from the Philippine insurrection about 120 years ago, right through to Fallujah. Every time we face a uniformed opponent, from the Spanish War right through the Cold War, and one might even say the initial part of the war against Saddam Hussein, it has been a heroic experience for our military. And so it is not surprising that they are focused on how to recreate a situation where their primary adversary is a uniformed state. But the real threats that we face are asymmetric, and they don't come from China.

Many of my colleagues in this room have had to listen to all of my hawkish comments about our trade relationship with China, and now they have had to listen to my dovish comments about these—they are called islands, but really islets or reefs that are in dispute. I think we have to assert freedom of navigation, but we also have to just calm everybody down.

And, finally, I would point out that none of the countries that claim these islets are willing to put the kind of money into defending them that they want us to. Japan continues to stick to 1 percent of its GDP. Our expenditure, as a percentage of GDP, is understated, because we don't include veterans benefits, but that is part of the compensation package of our soldiers and sailors.

So we are spending far more of our treasure and risking our lives around the world, and I would hope that our friends in Asia would figure out a way to just lower the temperature in all of this.

I yield back.

Mr. PERRY. The Chair thanks the ranking member.

In the interest of time, it would be good order just to make sure that the subcommittee is or will come to order. And, at this time, the Chair will now recognize itself for an opening statement. And, as a reminder, without objection, the members of the subcommittee can present brief remarks if they choose to, or they can submit them for the record.

Overlapping territorial claims to the South China Sea have been a source of international friction since 2009. And it is no secret that China's claim and actions in the region have been the most aggressive. No one would have guessed that submerged features, rocks, and tiny islets seen here—if we can get the photos up, please—seen here, would be a source of major tension that it is today.

During previous hearing, Ranking Member Sherman has asked a good question. Why should these rocks and any resources that might be under them matter to the United States? It is true that these features are themselves insignificant, but the outcome of these disputes will decide questions much more important than who owns what number of ocean rocks and sand, especially if other countries are building airstrips and radar towers on them.

The region is flush with trade routes, fishing areas, and untold potential natural and energy resources. Protecting the freedom of the seas for commerce and passage while also protecting smaller states and U.S. allies from being coerced is absolutely a U.S. priority.

U.S. leadership in the South China Sea is sorely needed. We stand alone as a world power, and our ability to engage China on complex issues for which there are no easy solutions, yet our leadership is noticeably absent and inconsistent. Today we will look into how the United States can help keep the world's oceans free and open and how China's activity in the South China Sea affects our bilateral relationship.

We cannot let Beijing unilaterally define new norms of behavior at the expense of regional stability and the principles and goals of global development and international law. China, with its infamous Nine-Dash Line, which is now shown on the screen, claims virtually the entirety of the South China Sea has been the most aggressive and notorious of all South China Sea claimants.

While China's intentions remain deliberately unclear, its actions, including the construction of artificial islands, the apparent use of these features for military purposes, the placing of oil rigs in disputed waters, and the flooding of the region with military and civilian ships are clearly aimed at asserting itself as a maritime power, but inconsistent with international law and norms of behavior.

While China has signaled that they would halt land reclamation, China will continue to construct facilities on the features. I hope to hear from our panel of experts as to what China might do with these facilities. Beijing's remarks about halting land reclamation were also timed to coincide with high-level discussions, and experts have already discounted the sincerity of China's stated intentions.

Besides superficial concessions, what else can the United States do to prevent China's monopoly on international waters? Other nations laying claim to disputed South China Sea territory, including Vietnam, the Philippines, Malaysia, and Brunei, some—that was a period at the end of that. Some claimants have also used questionable tactics to state claims to disputed territories. But while China may argue it is only playing catch-up to these smaller nations' history of territory grabs, the speed and scale of China's activities is unparalleled.

Chinese aggression in the South China Sea threatens regional and global security and stability, as well as the peaceful international system of the rule of law and freedom of navigation and overflight.

U.S. Pacific Fleet Commander Admiral Scott Swift recently expressed that American forces are well equipped and ready to respond to any contingency in the South China Sea. While our allies have requested U.S. support and assistance in the region, they may not be holding their breath. The Philippines has already proposed a 25 percent increase of its defense budget for 2016. Vietnam increased its defense budget by 9.6 percent in 2014.

With unprecedented increases in defense budgets within the region, is Southeast Asia facing an impending and widespread arms race? What role does the U.S. have in tempering this escalation? The Obama administration and leading experts have all echoed concerns about developments in the South China Sea, yet U.S. and regional responses have been ineffective in curtailing Chinese expansion. No one involved in these disputes wants a military conflict, but the United States must continue to protect and preserve the principle of freedom of the seas, while supporting a peaceful resolution of competing territorial claims based on international law.

I remain concerned about activity in the South China Sea, how regional developments may undermine stability, and about the lack of a unified U.S. voice in assuring the freedom of the seas. We need a clear strategy to address the South China Sea. It is my hope that our panel will help to develop this framework. For our country to forego or complicate this responsibility is a failure of conscience, history, and national will.

Again, members present will be permitted to submit written statements to be included in the official hearing record. Without objection, the hearing record will remain open for 5 calendar days to allow statements, questions, and extraneous material for the record, subject to the length of the limitations in the rules.

And, at this time, that concludes the Chairman's opening statement, and I will recognize other members for their opening statements. Mr. Bera, the gentleman from California.

Mr. BERA. Yes. I thank the chairman. I am going to respectfully disagree with my colleague from California, Mr. Sherman, in the sense that I do think this is an incredibly serious, you know, issue that we need to take up and we have taken up both in this subcommittee as well as discussed in the full committee.

You know, these are incredibly important trading routes and will become more important as, you know, we increase our trade and commerce within the Asia Pacific region. China's moves both in the East China Sea and Senkaku Islands, as well as, you know, their moves here in the South China Sea, do need to be addressed and need to be addressed in a way that makes China understand that there are normal rules of negotiation in terms of when there are disagreements like what we are seeing in the South China Sea, and those dispute resolution processes have to take these standards of normal dispute resolution.

In addition, you know, my concern is, as they gain a foothold, as they build airfields, you know, as they move additional vessels into the region, it is going to be much more difficult to—you know, to dislodge this, and it does set a very bad precedent for a region. You know, I am very interested in hearing the testimony of the experts, what our options are.

You know, nobody on this subcommittee believes that an armed resolution is the right way to go. You know, we firmly believe, you know, we should be able to resolve this diplomatically, but we should resolve this diplomatically under the normal rules of negotiation.

In addition, the one thing that I do worry about is, as Vietnam, as the Philippines, as other nations that, you know, express some claims on these waters put more vessels in the water, more ships, the chance of an accidental incident—and we have seen some of the incidents between China and Vietnam—for an accidental incident to escalate becomes a real danger. And that is how we end up in an armed conflict, and that is something that we very much want to avoid.

I think I have heard that the United States is continuing to disregard the fly zones, which I wholeheartedly accept. Again, you know, these are open zones for, you know, our planes to fly through, and they should continue to be open internationally recognized zones for both shipping and air travel.

So, again, I am very interested in hearing the committee's testimony. I am certainly interested in hearing the witnesses' thoughts on various options, but I do think we have to speak as a strong, unified voice, and, you know, it is important for the United States to speak as still the sole superpower, as a superpower that has very important allies in the region. And as we start to set the rules of commerce for the Asia Pacific region, you know, setting those standards is going to be very important.

So, again, I look forward to the testimony, and I will yield back.

Mr. PERRY. The Chair thanks the gentleman.

The Chair now recognizes the gentlelady from New York, Ms. Meng.

Ms. MENG. Thank you, Mr. Chairman, Ranking Member Sherman, and all our witnesses for being here today. The South China Sea is a place of great strategic importance for many countries, including the United States. Five-point-three trillion dollars in commerce passes through the South China Sea every year, and stability in the region is vital to continuing economic connections and U.S. security interests.

Territorial disputes in the South China Sea test the stability of the region. The recent increase in maritime incidents is a concern, because with these incidents comes tension. It is important that the disputes be resolved peacefully. All parties involved should come to the table to negotiate a fair resolution to the conflict. The United States has taken a number of steps to ensure peace and stability in the region.

Thank you, and I yield back.

Mr. PERRY. The Chair thanks the gentlewoman.

Today, we are grateful to be joined by a panel of experts from the private sector who follow this issue closely. Dr. Patrick Cronin is a senior advisor and director of the Asia-Pacific Security Program at the Center for a New American Security. Dr. Andrew Erickson is an associate professor at the U.S. Naval War College, where he is a founding member of the China Maritime Studies Institute.

Dr. Mira Rapp-Hooper is a fellow in the Asia Program at the Center for Strategic and International Studies where she is director of the Asia Maritime Transparency Initiative. And Dr. Michael Swaine joins us from the Carnegie Endowment for International Peace where he is a senior associate in the Asia Program.

Thank you all for joining us. You will see a series of lights in front of you, so we would hope, if you could, to confine your testimony as closely to 5 minutes as you can, and you will see the lights coming down. And also, when you speak, of course, push the button to talk. And then, when you are done, push the button, so that you don't continue to be recorded when you don't want to be.

That having been said, we will now turn to Dr. Patrick Cronin for his testimony.

STATEMENT OF PATRICK M. CRONIN, PH.D., SENIOR ADVISOR AND SENIOR DIRECTOR, ASIA–PACIFIC SECURITY PROGRAM, CENTER FOR A NEW AMERICAN SECURITY

Mr. CRONIN. Mr. Chairman, Mr. Bera, thank you so much for the honor to testify on America's security role in the South China Sea. In the past several years, we have entered a period of intensified competition in the South China Sea. My view, maritime tensions are growing and will persist.

We may not be comfortable with the volatility that that persistence brings, but it is going to be a fact of life, in my judgment. And I think we can manage this below the threshold of military conflict. It is certainly important for the U.S. interest to do so.

But I think the reason the competition continues is largely because it is centered on China's reemergence as a major power, its capacity as a major power, and its desire to expand its influence over its neighbors and its adjacent waters in this century.

Now, the South China Sea is mostly not about rocks, reefs, and resources. It is about rules and order, the big order questions here. My written testimony enumerates eight essential elements of a U.S. foreign policy to deal with the South China Sea. They emphasize our enduring principles of unimpeded access to the global commons and peaceful resolution of disputes. They also include investing in America's own comprehensive power. This is really about our game. What do we bring to the region? Especially through regional trade and development, but also by enhancing our diplomatic and legal instruments of power.

The United States needs to deepen and broaden its diplomatic and practical support for the Association of Southeast Asian Nations, ASEAN. And we should bolster ASEAN-centered institutions on four levels, not just one, but four levels, with ASEAN as a whole, with ASEAN claimant states, with individual ASEAN members, and with maritime allies and partners in and outside of ASEAN, including Australia, India, Japan, and the Republic of Korea.

We should coalesce a maritime coalition of the willing to ensure that the South China Sea issues remain on the top of regional diplomacy. We can underscore rules and expectations as well as think through in advance a common response to perceived provocation such as a possible air defense identification zone. The United States should also support a regional transparency regime. I refer to not only the physical infrastructure for gathering information, but also the institutions to process it, and the political channels to share it, both within and between governments.

At the broadest level, by supporting greater transparency of developments in the South China Sea, we can help the region arm itself with facts to deal with everything from search and rescue to humanitarian assistance and disaster relief, to the fortification of islands, to threatening deployments of vessels.

Leveraging our relations with allies, like the Philippines and other like-minded states, the United States can build on this general information-sharing regime to create a higher fidelity common operating picture for both early warning and contingency response. The technical capacity to build such a regime already exist, but U.S. leadership will be needed to build the supporting political framework. Let us put the spotlight on these stabilizing actions, so that we can reinforce the diplomacy at high level, regional, and global gatherings.

The South China Sea is one area that needs more congressional fact-finding delegations, including to China. The United States should seek to clarify types of behavior that would be objectionable and against which the United States would work with others to impose costs. For instance, we should consider opposing the seizure of any unoccupied feature by denying access to other claimants, sovereignty claims over features that are not islands, spurious military alert zones. And I have a longer list in my written testimony

Finally, we should enumerate a menu of potential cost imposition policy options that transcend reputational and legal costs and make clear that bad behavior will incur a price. Congress should require the continuous development of such an options menu in a classified annex of future interagency regional strategism, but let me suggest just a few—multi-national sea and air patrols could emulate recent U.S. P–8 overflights to make an emphatic point about what is permitted under UNCLOS.

If a country wants to build an artificial island for military purposes in disputed waters, and then suggests it might be used for civilian purposes such as humanitarian assistance, then during the next regional disaster we might test that proposition by landing a civilian aircraft on one of the newest runways.

If China tries to prevent the resupply of BRP Sierra Madre at Ayungin Shoal, then the United States might not only offer to resupply that Philippine ship, but it could also consider deploying a few Marines on rotation as part of the crew's training detachment. These are pugnacious, but these would be in response to future bad behavior. These, and many other moves, are the kind of muscular punctuation points designed not to ignite conflict, but rather to clarify acceptable behavior and reinforce the kind of rule set the region should and can live by.

We are looking for an inclusive rules-based system with China. In the absence of any substantial costs for bad behavior, however, China will be emboldened to carry on with its opportunistic probing for regional influence. We need an effective counterweight to keep China honest, safeguard access to the global commons for all, and uphold the rule of law.

Thank you.

[The prepared statement of Mr. Cronin follows:]

America's Security Role in the South China Sea

Dr. Patrick M. Cronin
Senior Advisor and Senior Director, Asia-Pacific Security Program
Center for a New American Security

House Committee on Foreign Affairs
Subcommittee on Asia and the Pacific
2172 Rayburn House Office Building
July 23, 2015

Chairman Salmon, Ranking Member Sherman, and other distinguished Members of the Subcommittee on Asia and the Pacific, I am honored to have this opportunity to testify on America's security role in the South China Sea.

In the past several years, we have entered a period of intensified competition in the South China Sea. Maritime tensions in Asia are growing and will persist, and yet relations are likely to remain bounded below the threshold of military conflict. All sides are positioning to gain the upper hand and to minimize less advantageous positions. While we can still expect tactical maneuvering before and after summit meetings, strategic dialogues, and regional conferences, we should not expect tensions to fully subside. Despite calls for grand bargains and strategic accommodation, I believe that well into the next U.S. administration we will be navigating in the messy middle ground between war and peace. Although such volatility may be uncomfortable, achieving a firmer footing with China will likewise be difficult if not elusive. That is because the primary competition has a great deal to do with a reemerging China's capacity and desire for expanding its influence over its neighbors and adjacent waters, en route to securing a position as *a* if not *the* major global power in the 21st century.

The Asia-Pacific or Indo-Pacific region will offer some of the greatest opportunities and challenges for U.S. foreign policy in the decades ahead. In addressing what we need to do with respect to maritime territorial disputes in the South China Sea, the United States needs to place all of our foreign policy activities within a comprehensive framework designed to bring about future decades of stability, prosperity, and freedom.

Without attempting to write a regional strategy that would articulate important national interests and clear objectives, let me comment briefly on the rationale behind the U.S. policy of a long-term reorientation of our comprehensive power to the Indo-Pacific region. The driving force behind America's gradual rebalance to the Indo-Pacific is rooted in secular trends. For the first time since the 18th century, Asia is becoming the locus of the global economy and world politics. According to the National Intelligence Council, by 2030 Asia is projected to overtake both North America and Europe in terms of global power as measured by GDP, population, defense spending, and investment in technology. China has been the largest engine, but a more inclusive analysis shows that most of Asia has grown, is growing, and will keep growing.

The South China Sea is not just or even mostly about rocks, reefs, and resources. While some have likened China and the South China Sea to America and the Caribbean, such an analogy quickly loses its explanatory power because of the stark differences between the two bodies of water and changes in the global economy. Unlike the Caribbean in the mid-19th century, the South China Sea is at the nexus of the global economy. All maritime powers depend on it because through its waters sail half of the world's commercial shipping by tonnage (valued at more than $5.3 trillion). Furthermore, Southeast Asian nations comprise nearly two-thirds of a billion people with a GDP pushing $4 trillion in purchasing power parity; and there are great expectations for those economies in the decades ahead. Finally, we live in—or should at least strive to live in—a world governed by rules, not spheres of influence, such as those that may have been more in vogue in the 19th century. Thus, it is rules and order that remain at the heart of America's interests in Asia and the South China Sea.

Colleagues and at the Center for a New American Security (CNAS) began tracking China's recent pattern of assertiveness in 2009.[1]

Since then, China has transitioned from a hide-and-bide approach to greater activism in and beyond the South China Sea. While China has become marginally more transparent, in important areas it is as opaque as ever. As with China's expansive nine-dash-line claim to the South China Sea, there appear to be important areas of policy that China simply does not wish to clarify.

China's largely opportunistic push into the South China Sea is backed by an impressive array of military and non-military actions designed to exert greater control over its neighborhood. China is enhancing its strategic position through its incremental salami slicing tactics, which accrete to major changes to the status quo while warding off escalation. Its hasty island-building project is not just intended to change facts on the ground before international legal proceedings can run their course, but also to gain an upper hand over the region and intimidate neighbors into aligning with China. Consistent with China's non-kinetic "three warfares" (informational, legal, and psychological) doctrine, this positioning is a mixture of the physical and mental.

China continues to set the pace in regional defense spending with continuous, near-double-digit increases that now outpace the growth of the Chinese economy. Investments in ballistic and cruise missiles, for instance, are eroding America's previous advantage in precision strike systems. As a result, America's ability and perceived willingness to risk projecting power forward in defense of allies and partners is likely to be increasingly called into question unless the United States finds effective responses. China is also busy building many more cost-effective capabilities, military and non-military alike, to deny and ultimately control sea and air space, as well as cyber and outer space, in and around the South China Sea, East China Sea, and Taiwan Strait.

We, too, must step up the level of our activity to counter potential regional instability. At stake is whether the future order is built on fair and inclusive principles akin to those that have empowered China's and Asia's remarkable stability and prosperity. It is my judgment that the United States, working with allies and partners, can continue to realize its vision of an inclusive, stable, and rules-based order. Permit me to enumerate 10 essential elements of a U.S. foreign policy to deal with the South China Sea. They are intended to foster cooperation backed by clarity of purpose, fairness, and multidimensional strength.

First, the United States should regularly underscore our enduring principles for the South China Sea. As with our approach to unimpeded access throughout the global commons, the United States strives to strengthen the rule of law and uphold the peaceful settlement of disputes. Our officials should persist in spelling out America's positive vision for an inclusive, rules-based regional order. Customary international law and the United Nations Convention on the Law of the Sea should be fully respected, including the freedom of navigation through exclusive economic zones and the right of innocent passage in territorial seas. Furthermore, there should be no force or coercion to settle disputes, such as those that exist over the Spratly and Paracel Islands and Scarborough Reef. While the United States should remain neutral on sovereignty disputes, it has a responsibility to ensure that disputes should be revolved or managed without using force, threats of force, or coercion. Principles rooted in the rule of law and peaceful resolution of disputes should ideally be embedded within a comprehensive and coherent regional strategy.

Secondly, the United States should reinvest in our own long-term economic power, something that can be achieved in large part by intensifying our trade and development ties in the Asia-Pacific. Completing the Trans-Pacific Partnership can demonstrate America's ability to complete complex free-trade agreements and regional architectures. We need to be prepared to bring more economies, from the Philippines to the Republic of Korea, into TPP, the first major multilateral trade agreement with a heavy focus on the new economy based on information technology and services. The United States can use TPP to gain critical leverage vis-à-vis BRICS nations regarding future rules for trade.

We also need more energy, imagination, and resources to assemble a serious multilateral development initiative of our own. We can wait and see about how complementary China's Asian Infrastructure and Investment Bank (AIIB) and "One Belt, One Road" initiatives will be to existing Bretton Woods institutions and other development initiatives. Meanwhile, we can do far better on development than the patchwork quilt of the Lower Mekong Initiative. Congress should request from the current and future administration a development strategy that includes proposals for new initiatives. I have in mind a major international public-private partnership in support of human development in Asia. Rather than try to match China's push for physical infrastructure, I would focus on the new knowledge economy, human capital and education, science and technology, and energy—all areas of comparative advantage for the United States.

Thirdly, the United States needs to deepen and broaden its diplomatic and practical support for the Association of Southeast Asian Nations (ASEAN). ASEAN centrality has already been a key tenet of the U.S. approach to regional multilateral architecture. But the United States should do more to achieve ASEAN unity and bolster ASEAN-centered institutions on at least four levels: with ASEAN as a whole, with ASEAN claimant states, with individual ASEAN member states, and with maritime allies and partners in and outside of ASEAN (including Australia, India, Japan, and the Republic of Korea). On the initial level, the United States should continue to seek to preserve ASEAN consensus over the norms related to the rule of law and peaceful resolution of disputes. Key partners such as Singapore and Indonesia can be instrumental, but so, too, can our longstanding ally Thailand, which is the ASEAN coordinator for outreach to China.

Working to achieve ASEAN unity over basic principles is useful, but the United States can find more effective diplomatic traction by forging a stronger caucus among claimant states. Hence, fourthly, the United States should help the ASEAN claimants (not just the Philippines and Vietnam, but also Malaysia and Brunei) to come to a common understanding and work towards a common goal that is fair to all countries. They can reduce differences, set forth common expectations for conduct, and forge cooperative approaches to diplomacy and security. These do not necessarily entail the resolution of the sovereignty and all jurisdictional disputes, which is in any case not possible without the participation of China, but they could conceivably reflect principles that hew to the rule of law and peaceful resolution of disputes. China has tried to inhibit the formation of a regional consensus by slowing down processes such as the Code of Conduct negotiations between it and ASEAN. A viable consensus among the ASEAN maritime caucus could break this logjam. At the same time, the United States should help ASEAN claimant states to work towards that common goal by giving support in areas such as diplomacy, facilitation, legal expertise, and, as I will amplify below, operational capability.

A fifth recommended action is to build a maritime coalition of the willing to ensure that South China Sea issues remain on the top tier of regional diplomacy. The United States should leverage ASEAN's convening power to bring together a wider coalition of maritime powers. Key members would include Japan, Australia and India, all of whom understand that the South China Sea is a vital part of the global economy and not just one big country's pond. We can underscore rules and expectations, as well as think through in advance a common response to perceived provocations such as a possible declaration of an Air Defense Identification Zone (ADIZ) in the South China Sea. Thus, from ASEAN Regional Forum ministers' meetings to more inclusive diplomatic institutions such as the East Asia Summit process and the ASEAN Defense Ministers' Meeting Plus, the United States should insist on elevating the South China Sea issue to the highest priority to discourage China from taking assertive and counterproductive actions in the South China Sea.

Sixth, the United States should maintain a constant presence in the South China Sea. Singapore has enabled a steady if quiet presence, most recently by hosting up to four littoral combat ships. Additional disbursement of capabilities and the creation of additional access agreements, including for extended rotational tours, such as those envisaged in the Philippines and already announced in Australia, can reinforce our commitment to stability and engagement. Completing a buildup on Guam and the Marianas, though outside the South China Sea, can provide a tremendous opportunity for region-wide exercising and training of maritime, air, and coast guard forces. I believe these steps are consistent with the intent of the military dimension of the U.S. rebalance to Asia.

Seventh, the United States should support an overlapping regional transparency regime that serves multiple objectives. A transparency regime refers to not only physical infrastructure for gathering information but also the institutions to process it and the political channels to share it, both within and between governments. At the broadest level, by supporting greater transparency of developments in the South China Sea, we can help the region arm itself with facts to deal with everything from search and rescue or humanitarian assistance and disaster relief, to the fortification of artificial islands or provocative deployments of vessels. Leveraging our relations with allies such as the Philippines and other like-minded states, the United States can build on this general information-sharing regime to create a higher fidelity common operating picture for early warning and contingency response. The technical capacity to build such a regime already exists, but U.S. leadership will be needed to build the supporting political framework. Let's put the spotlight on destabilizing actions so that we can reinforce the diplomacy at high-level regional and global gatherings.

The South China Sea region is one area that needs more Congressional fact-finding delegations. Visits through the region should include China, where listening to different points of view might be helpful in sparking a wider discussion and gradually building shared understanding.

Eighth, in addition to building maritime domain awareness, we should also be building national and multinational defensive and deterrent capacity for supporting assured access throughout the South China Sea. The broader maritime coalition alluded to above could undertake periodic, perhaps even quarterly, air and sea patrols in the South China Sea to review developments up close as well as to provide a capacity to respond to all hazards, ranging from the non-traditional to more traditional security risks. The aim of such capacity is defensive, offering smaller countries reassurance and hopefully deterring acts of aggression and unilateral changes to the status quo through force.

Ninth, the United States should seek to clarify types of behavior that would be objectionable and against which the United States would work with others to impose costs. Harkening back to the basic principles and the desire to strengthen U.S. presence and regional engagement, the United States should make clear that it opposes and will continue to oppose certain specific types of activities throughout the South China Sea. The precise details should be thoroughly vetted by a beefed-up cadre of government experts on international maritime law. But for illustrative purposes, let me suggest the following types of actions we should consider opposing: (a) blockading any feature occupied by another claimant, such as Second Thomas Shoal occupied by the Philippines; (b) seizing or encroaching on any feature occupied by another claimant, such as China's seizure of the western half of the Paracels from South Vietnam in 1974 and of Johnson South Reef from Vietnam in 1988; (c) the encroachment on the territorial sea of any island occupied by another claimant; (d) the seizure of any unoccupied feature by denying access to other claimants, such as China's current exclusion of Philippine nationals from Scarborough Reef; (e) the creation of artificial islands and the enlargement of either natural or artificial islands; (f) sovereignty claims over features that are not islands, i.e., those that are not naturally above high tide, or over low-tide-elevations that are more than 12 nautical miles from islands, such as Mischief Reef and Subi Reef; (g) baseline claims that are not UNCLOS compliant; (h) claims to territorial sea or EEZ from baselines that are not UNCLOS compliant, such as those based on low-tide elevations or artificial islands that are more than 12 nautical miles from islands; (i) claims to maritime space that is excessive according to international law on maritime delimitation, such as China's claims to the maritime space inside the nine-dash line; (j) claims to maritime space that are not derived from land or insular territories, such as China's claims to historic rights over the area inside the nine-dash line; (k) spurious military alert zones, such as that established over the deep-sea oil platform HD-981 or in the case of U.S. Navy P-8 Poseidon overflights; and (l) the establishment of ADIZs over the disputed features and their waters.

Tenth, we should enumerate a menu of potential cost-imposition policy options that transcend reputational and legal costs and make clear that bad behavior will incur a price. Congress should require the continuous development of such an options menu in a classified annex of future interagency regional strategies. Multinational sea and air patrols could emulate recent U.S. P-8 overflights to make an emphatic point about what is permitted under UNCLOS. Similarly, if a country wants to build an artificial island for military purposes in disputed waters and then suggest it might be used for civilian purposes such as humanitarian assistance, then during the next regional disaster we might test that proposition by landing a civilian aircraft on one of the newest runways. If China tries to prevent the resupply of the grounded Philippine naval vessel BRP Sierra Madre at Ayungin Shoal, then the United States might not only offer to resupply it, but could also consider deploying a few Marines on rotation as part of the crew's training detachment. These and many other moves are the kind of muscular punctuation points designed not to ignite conflict but rather to clarify acceptable and unacceptable behavior and reinforce the kind of rule set the region should and can live by.

Let me sum up my argument. Growing tensions in the South China Sea are threatening to arrest one of the most significant developments in modern history: namely, the rise of Asia and the largely U.S.-created order on which stability and prosperity rest. China's assertive reemergence is challenging regional stability. Its rapid military modernization, frequent resort to tailored coercion, and artificial-island-*cum*-military-base-building program in the South China Sea directly undermine both the post-World War II order and American credibility. China's use of all instruments of power and incremental salami slicing tactics are out-maneuvering the competition. China is gradually *de-balancing* the region; in the absence of any substantial cost for bad behavior, China is simply being emboldened to carry on with its opportunistic and aggressive probing for regional influence. Without an effective counterweight to keep China honest, safeguard freedom of navigation and access to the global commons for all, and uphold the rule of law, China will achieve a slow-motion hegemony throughout the South China Sea. This testimony has provided some of the practical and comprehensive policy steps that the United States might act upon to protect the interests of the United States, as well as its allies in partners, for decades to come.

---

[1] See Patrick M. Cronin and Alexander Sullivan, *Preserving the Rules: Countering Coercion in Maritime Asia* (Washington, D.C.: CNAS, March 2015); Ely Ratner et al., *More Willing & Able: Charting China's International Activism* (Washington, D.C.: CNAS, May 2015); Patrick M. Cronin et al., *Tailored Coercion: Competition and Risk in Maritime Asia* (Washington, D.C.: CNAS, March 2014); and Patrick M. Cronin, editor, *Cooperation from Strength: The United States, China and the South China Sea* (Washington, D.C.: CNAS, January 2012). All are available and can be viewed or downloaded at www.cnas.org.

15

Mr. PERRY. The Chair thanks Dr. Cronin for his testimony and now recognizes Dr. Erickson for his testimony.

STATEMENT OF ANDREW S. ERICKSON, PH.D., ASSOCIATE PROFESSOR, CHINA MARITIME STUDIES INSTITUTE, U.S. NAVAL WAR COLLEGE

Mr. ERICKSON. Mr. Chairman, Mr. Bera, in 2014, China started developing land features in the Spratlys and Paracels, with scale and sophistication its neighbors simply can't match, even collectively over time. But most concerning is what China is constructing there—militarily relevant facilities, including two 3,000-meter runways capable of serving manifold military aircraft.

No other South China Sea claimant enjoys even one runway of this caliber on the features it occupies. One logical application for China's current activities: Supporting a South China Sea air defense identification zone, or ADIZ, like the one Beijing announced over the East China Sea in November 2013.

The way China announced its East China Sea ADIZ suggests that it is reserving the right to treat international airspace beyond 12 nautical miles as territorial airspace in important respects. My colleague Peter Dutton characterizes China's island-building and outfitting activities as a tipping point meriting U.S. response. Militarizing the newly constructed islands, he argues persuasively, will alter strategic stability and the regional balance of power.

Recent activities exemplify broader concerns—that as it becomes increasingly powerful China will abandon previous restraint, bully smaller neighbors, threaten use of force to resolve disputes, and attempt to change—or else run roughshod over—important international norms that preserve peace in Asia and which underwrite the global system on which mutual prosperity depends.

That is why the U.S. now needs to adjust thinking and policy to stabilize the situation and balance against the prospect of negative Chinese behavior and influence. Even as China advances, we cannot retreat. The South China Sea is a vital part of the global commons on which the international system depends. Many statistics have already been offered to support that very important point.

We therefore cannot allow Beijing to carve out within these international waters and airspace a zone of exceptionalism in which its neighbors face bullying without recourse, and vital global rules and norms are subordinated to Beijing's parochial priorities. Instead, we must maintain the national will and force structure to continue to operate in, under, and over the South China Sea, East China Sea, and Yellow Sea, and to preserve them as peaceful parts of the global commons for all to use without fear.

There, given China's growing power and our own sustained power and resolve, we must accept a zone of managed strategic friction and contestation. China's current leadership is clearly comfortable with a certain level of tension, and we must be, too. This includes accepting the fundamental reality that we won't roll back China's existing occupation of islands and other features, just as we won't accept China's rolling back of its neighbors' own occupation.

Most fundamentally, the U.S. must preserve peace and a stable status quo in a vital yet vulnerable region that remains haunted by history. To this end, we must develop and maintain a force structure and a set of supporting policies and partnerships geared to ensuring access, despite Chinese development of counter-intervention capabilities.

We must make particular effort to preserve the significant U.S. advantage in undersea warfare by emphasizing nuclear-powered attack submarines and offensive naval mines. If we are not building at least two Virginia-class submarines per year, we are not being serious, and regional allies, partners, and China will see that clearly.

We must also take a page from China's counter-intervention playbook and further prioritize anti-ship cruise missiles. Unless we close this very real missile gap, China is poised to outstick the U.S. Navy by 2020 by deploying greater quantities of missiles with greater ranges than those of the U.S. ship-based systems able to defend against them.

Let me be clear: The U.S. and China can, and will I believe, avoid war. Rather, this is about maintaining robust deterrence in peacetime and in any crises that might erupt. Specifically, we must deter Beijing from attempting to resolve island or maritime claims disputes with the use of force or even the threat of force.

The aforementioned weapon systems, effectively deployed and combined with a broader strategy, can repeatedly convince China's leaders that they won't succeed in their objective if they attempt to use military force to seize additional features in waters around them, or to prevent U.S. forces from operating in international waters and airspace nearby.

Thank you very much.

[The prepared statement of Mr. Erickson follows:]

23 July 2015

Andrew S. Erickson

Associate Professor

China Maritime Studies Institute

U.S. Naval War College

Testimony before the House Committee on Foreign Affairs

Subcommittee on Asia and the Pacific

Hearing on

America's Security Role in the South China Sea

This statement reflects solely the author's personal views.
It does not reflect the policies or estimates of the U.S. Navy, the U.S. Naval War College,
or any other organization of the U.S. Government.

Chairman Salmon, Ranking Member Sherman, and distinguished members of the subcommittee, thank you for this opportunity to address this vital, timely topic. Allow me to share my assessment of the current situation in the South China Sea, followed by my recommendations concerning how the U.S. government should understand the situation and how it may best work to address it.

Emerging Situation

A major Chinese narrative regarding the South China Sea is one of unreciprocated restraint. But Chinese leaders have clearly had an ambitious long-term vision of some sort, backed by years of efforts, themselves based on longstanding claims encapsulated in an ambiguous "nine-dash line" enclosing virtually all of the South China Sea.

Beijing's stance regarding South China Sea sovereignty issues is categorical and steadfast. In a position paper rejecting outright the Philippines' recent initiation of international arbitration regarding their bilateral dispute, China's Ministry of Foreign Affairs states, "China has indisputable sovereignty over the South China Sea Islands (the Dongsha [Pratas] Islands, Xisha [Paracel] Islands, the Zhongsha Islands [whose main features include Macclesfield Bank and Scarborough Shoal] and the Nansha [Spratly] Islands) and the adjacent waters."[1]

Despite all its rhetoric, actions, developmental efforts, and apparent preparations, however, China has repeatedly declined to disclose the precise basis for, the precise nature of, or even the precise geographical parameters of, its South China Sea claims. As the U.S. Office of Naval Intelligence documents, China "has never published the coordinates of" the nine-dash line that it draws around virtually the entire South China Sea—perilously close to the coasts of its neighbors, all of whom it has disputes with. It has not "declared what rights it purports to enjoy in this area."[2] Beijing has still has not specified whether or not it considers the South China Sea to constitute a "core interest." Given China's statements and actions to date, however, there is reason for concern that it is determined to maintain expansive claims based on unyielding invocation of the "nine-dash line."

Island Seizure History

China's military and paramilitary forces have a half-century-plus history of capturing islands and other features, many in South China Sea. It appears that Beijing long harbored ambitions to seize significant numbers of South China Sea islands, and indeed took several occupied by Vietnam in 1974 and 1988 even though severely limited in sea and air power at that time. Such operations have not received sufficient analytical attention. In some respects, they may have been more complex that previously appreciated outside China. For example. maritime militia forces appear to have been employed in the 1974 Paracels Conflict,[3] the 2009 Impeccable Incident, the 2012 Scarborough Shoal Standoff,[4] and the 2014 Haiyang Shiyou 981 Oil Rig Standoff.[5] It is important to note that in none of these cases—or in recent Chinese cutting of the cables of Vietnamese oil and gas survey vessels or Chinese intimidation of Philippine forces at Second Thomas Shoal—did the United States intervene to stop Chinese actions.

Regarding the abovementioned cases that occurred since the end of the Cold War, this is. in part. because Washington does not take a position on the relative validity of South China Sea countries' sovereignty claims *per se*. Instead, what the U.S. opposes consistently is (1) the use of force, or the threat of force, to resolve such disputed claims; and (2) attempts to limit freedom of navigation or other vital international system-sustaining norms.[6]

Industrial-scale Island Construction

That brings us to recent events, which I believe have precipitated today's hearing—and rightly so. In 2014, China greatly accelerated what had long been a very modest process of "island building," developing land features in the Spratlys and Paracels on with a scale and sophistication that its neighbors simply cannot match, even collectively over time.[7] "Features," is the key word here, because many were previously small rocks or reefs not legally considered "islands." Then China used some of the world's largest dredgers to build up some of the most pristine coral reefs above water with thousands of tons of sand, coral cuttings, and concrete. U.S. Pacific Fleet Commander Admiral Harry Harris aptly terms China's creation a "Great Wall of Sand." It has created over 2,000 acres of "land" where none remained above South China Sea waters before. But it's what China is constructing atop this artificial edifice that most concerns its neighbors and the United States: militarily relevant facilities, including at least two runways capable of serving a wide range of military aircraft, that could allow Beijing to exert increasing influence over the South China Sea.

Beijing *itself* has stated officially that there will be military uses for the new "islands" it has raised from the sea. On 9 March 2015, China Foreign Ministry spokeswoman Hua Chunying stated that Spratly garrison "maintenance and construction work" was intended in part for *"better safeguarding territorial sovereignty and maritime rights and interests."*[8] Hua elaborated that construction was designed in part to *"satisfy the necessary military defense needs."* Chinese military sources employ similar wording.

The likely translation, in concrete terms:
- better facilities for personnel stationed on the features
- port facilities for logistics, maritime militia, coast guard, and navy ships
- a network of radars to enable monitoring of most of the South China Sea
- air defense missiles
- airstrips for civilian and military aircraft

Then-Commander of the U.S. Pacific Command Admiral Samuel Locklear's 15 April 2015 testimony before the House Armed Services Committee supports this assessment: In addition to basing Chinese Coast Guard ships to expand influence over a contested area, "expanded land features down there also could eventually lead to the deployment of things, such as long-range radars, military and advanced missile systems…" Locklear added: "it might be a platform for them, if they ever wanted to establish an [Air Defense Identification Zone/ADIZ] for them to be able to enforce that from."

Airstrips… and ADIZ?

For airstrips, after structural integrity, it's length that matters most. There's no need for a 3,000 m runway (as China now has on Woody Island and Fiery Cross Reef) to support evacuation of personnel for medical or weather emergencies via turboprop and other civilian aircraft. Such a runway is only need to support a full range of military options. Building a separate taxiway alongside, as China has already done at Fiery Cross Reef, suggests plans for high tempo, high sortie rate military operations. No other South China Sea claimant enjoys even one runway of this caliber on any of the features that it occupies.

One logical application for China's current activities: to support a South China Sea ADIZ. Beijing announced an ADIZ in the East China Sea in November 2013. Many nations—including the United States—have established such zones to track aircraft approaching their territorial airspace (out to 12 nautical miles from their coast), particularly aircraft apparently seeking to enter that space.[9]

Radars on China-controlled features can form a network providing maritime/air domain awareness for the majority of the South China Sea. Fighter aircraft can allow China to intercept foreign aircraft it detects operating there, particularly those that do not announce their presence, or otherwise engage in behaviors that Beijing deems objectionable.

But while any coastal state is legally entitled to announce an ADIZ, the way in which China has done so in the East China Sea is worrisome. China threatens still-unspecified "defensive emergency measures" if foreign aircraft don't comply with its orders—orders that an ADIZ does not give it license to issue or enforce physically. This suggests that China is reserving the "right" to treat *international* airspace beyond 12 nautical miles as "*territorial*" airspace" in important respects.

China's record on maritime sovereignty fuels this concern. The *vast* majority of nations agree that under international law a country with a coastline controls *only* economic resources in waters 12 to 200 nautical miles out—and even less if facing a neighbor's coast less than 400 nm away. But China additionally claims rights to control military activities in that "Exclusive Economic Zone," as well as, apparently, in the airspace above it.

China currently lacks long-range capable anti-submarine warfare (ASW) assets akin to U.S. P-3 and P-8 aircraft. The more "islands" it builds, even if only with helicopter pads (as opposed to full runways), the more it can increase helicopter-based ASW coverage of the South China Sea. In this way, distribution of Chinese-held features could compensate for ASW helicopters' "short legs." China could thereby attempt to start to negate one of the last remaining major U.S. Navy advantages—submarines—and possibly pursue a bastion strategy for its nuclear-powered ballistic missile submarines (SSBNs) in the South China Sea.

Tipping Point

My Naval War College colleague, China Maritime Studies Institute (CMSI) Director Peter Dutton, characterizes the aforementioned Chinese activities as a "tipping point" meriting U.S. government response. "Militarization of the newly constructed islands," he argues cogently, which China appears determined to do, will alter strategic stability and the regional balance of power. "It will turn the South China Sea into a strategic strait under threat of land-based power."[10] This is part of a "regional maritime strategy…to expand China's interior to cover the maritime domain under an umbrella of continental control."[11] Dutton contends, and I agree, that Beijing's militarization of artificial islands "sets the clock back to a time when raw power was the basis for dispute resolution. China's power play, combined with its refusal to arbitrate, its aversion to multilateral negotiations, and its refusal to enter into bilateral negotiations on the basis of equality, undermines regional stability and weakens important global institutions."[12]

As bad as things are already, they could get worse—particularly if American attention and resolve are in question. In attempting to prevent China from using military force to resolve island and maritime claims disputes in the South China Sea, the United States will increasingly face Beijing's three-pronged trident designed precisely to preserve such a possibility. Maritime militia and Coast Guard forces will be forward deployed, possibly enveloping disputed features as part of a "Cabbage Strategy"[13] that dares the U.S. military to use force against non-military personnel. Such forces would be supported by a deterrent backstop that includes both China's navy and its "anti-navy" of land-based anti-access/area denial (A2/AD), or "counter-intervention," forces, collectively deploying the world's largest arsenal of ballistic and cruise missiles. In the region, only Vietnam also has a maritime militia, and the U.S. Coast Guard is not positioned to oppose China's. Meanwhile, China's Coast Guard is already larger than those of all its neighbors combined, and still growing rapidly.[14]

More broadly, worries about China's island construction, developing force posture in the South China Sea, and accompanying official statements exemplify broader foreign concern about China's rise—that as it becomes increasingly powerful, Beijing will:

- abandon previous restraint in word and deed
- bully its smaller neighbors
- implicitly or explicitly threaten the use of force to resolve disputes
- and attempt to change—or else run roughshod over—important international norms that preserve peace in Asia and underwrite the global system on which mutual prosperity depends

China's combination of resolve, ambiguity, activities, and deployments has corrosive implications for regional stability and international norms. That's why the United States now needs to adjust conceptual thinking and policy to stabilize the situation and balance against the prospect of negative Chinese behavior and influence.

The Need for a Paradigm Shift

As Peter Dutton has long emphasized, the way forward for the United States is clear: *even as China advances, we cannot retreat.* Together with the East China Sea and the Yellow Sea, the South China Sea is a vital part of the global commons, on which the international system depends to operate effectively and equitably. Half of global commerce and 90% of regional energy imports transit the South China Sea alone. We cannot allow Beijing to carve out within these international waters and airspace a zone of exceptionalism in which its neighbors face bullying without recourse and vital global rules and norms are subordinated to its parochial priorities. This would set back severely what Beijing itself terms "democracy/democratization in international relations."[15] Instead, we must maintain the national will and force structure to continue to operate in, under, and over the South China, East China, and Yellow Seas; and preserve them as peaceful parts of the global commons for all to use without fear.

Accepting Moderate Friction

Here, given China's growing power and our own sustained power and resolve, we must accept a zone of bounded strategic friction and contestation. Such friction is manageable, and we must manage it. To do so effectively, we should develop the mindset that we are in a great power relationship wherein we need to act to protect our vital interests and support the global system even as China is working to promote its own vital interests. It means preparing to live in the same strategic space together, with overlapping vital interests. This is the essence of great power relations, reflecting a reversion to historical norms after the brief and unsustainable unipolar moment is over; even as the United States remains strong as the world's leading power, and the world remains far from being a true "multipolar" system.[16]

This robust but realistic approach includes accepting the fundamental reality that we will not roll back China's existing occupation of islands and other features, just as we will not accept its rolling back its neighbors' occupation of other islands and features. Most fundamentally, the United States must preserve peace and a stable status quo in a vital yet vulnerable region that remains haunted by history.

Embracing Competitive Coexistence

The paradigm we need to think about is a form of great power relations that I term "competitive coexistence."[17] It is not a comprehensive rivalry, as between the United States and the Soviet Union in the Cold War. Hence, charges that it constitutes a "containment strategy" driven by a "Cold War mentality" would be inaccurate. Rather, it has specific competitive aspects that we should not exacerbate gratuitously, yet must not shy away from. China's current leadership is clearly comfortable with a certain level of friction and tension. Given the current unfortunate circumstances, for the foreseeable future we too must accept, and make clear that we are comfortable with, a certain level of friction and tension.

The above paradigm has important implications for both U.S. rhetoric and policy. First, American officials must recognize what their Chinese counterparts have long understood: words matter. The United States must not appear to embrace Chinese policy concepts or formulations that make us appear to fear tension, or to be willing to yield to Beijing's principled policy positions in order to mitigate it. Such optics would only encourage Chinese testing and assertiveness vis-à-vis Washington and its regional allies. Accordingly, two particularly problematic formulations favored by Beijing (and their variants) must be banished from the lexicon of American official discourse:

1. "The Thucydides Trap"
2. "New-Type Great Power Relations"

Avoiding Thucydides Claptrap

As invoked by none other than Xi Jinping himself to pressure U.S. counterparts,[18] as well as by influential Chinese public intellectuals to call for U.S. concessions,[19] the idea of the imperative to avoid a "Thucydides Trap" represents a misapplication of history. It falsely implies that only by taking drastic measures can the United States and China avoid previous patterns of ruinous conflict between an established power and a rising power. The product of a time that human progress over the past century has finally rendered obsolete, Thucydides offers a cynical, outdated interpretation that has no place in American values, or the world that the United States seeks to promote: "The strong do what they can, while the weak suffer what they must." I'm confident that's not the kind of world we're here to promote today.

Nor *should* we. As Thomas Christensen argues persuasively in his new book *The China Challenge*—already recognized as one of the leading works on U.S.-China relations—however, the evolution of nuclear weapons, international institutions, globalization, financial markets, and trans-national production chains have made the world a very different place than it was just over a century ago in 1914 when the Great War erupted.[20] Washington and Beijing certainly face friction, tensions, and even the possibility of future crises of some severity, but significant shared interests—economic and otherwise—as well as collective reliance on a dynamic international system, together with mutual deterrence, will enable them to avoid war. Both sides are restrained by these strong positive and negative incentives; it is not necessary for Washington to shoulder the burden of restraint alone. Instead, raising false hopes in Beijing only to have them dashed disappointingly is significantly more dangerous than being clear and firm from the start. U.S. policy makers must thus consistently avoid embracing flawed historical analogies that encourage unrealistic expectations on Beijing's part. Such dangerous "claptrap" must be relegated to the dustbin of history, where it truly belongs.

To set the right tone and expectations while safeguarding U.S. interests, the Chinese policy bumper sticker that flows from falling for the "Thucydides Trap" must likewise be rejected. As originated and promoted by Beijing, the concept of "New-Type Great Power Relations"[21] is invoked to imply that Washington must respect China's "core interests" (including, apparently, in the South China Sea) while not committing Beijing to corresponding accommodation in return.[22] As one Japanese contact asked me pointedly, "Why would you choose to wrestle in China's own sumo ring?"

Why indeed? Instead, the United States should proactively and consistently promote its own policy formulations. Robert Zoellick's "responsible stakeholder" concept is an excellent example, and it was a serious mistake for the Obama Administration to cede the field in this competition of ideas. To the extent that Beijing opposes the idea of responsibilities being thrust upon it, I propose that "strategic stakeholder" might be a better phrase. In any case, each side is free to employ its own concepts and rhetoric. But, at a minimum, the policy formulations that we ourselves embrace should at least meet the standard of the Hippocratic Oath of international relations: "first, do no harm." That typically means using our own wording unless there is a compelling reason to do otherwise.

Specific Policy Recommendations

As for substantive efforts, we must develop and maintain a force structure and set of supporting policies and partnerships geared to ensuring access despite Chinese development of counter-intervention capabilities. Even maintaining mutual deterrence vis-à-vis China could be good enough for the United States—Washington's key objective is to prevent the use, or threat, of force to resolve regional disputes. But allowing even the perception that such ability to "hold the ring" has eroded could gravely threaten the stability of a vibrant yet vulnerable region. Key questions for consideration thus include:

- What systems do we need to develop and acquire?
- How should we engage our military and other government forces to act?
- What risks must we accept?
- What should we ask of our allies and security partners in support?

In addition to cooperation and capacity building with regional allies and partners, the United States must maintain robust deterrence that paces China's growing arsenal of counter-intervention weapons. Here, unfortunately, Washington continues to suffer lingering effects from mishandling of the Iraq War and its aftermath. Among other problems, a decade of land wars with unclear, unrealistic objectives diverted attention and resources from capabilities to preserve the ability of the U.S. military to operate in maritime East Asia even while threatened by Chinese systems. Washington is finally devoting increased attention to several types of weapons with particular potential to demonstrate that counter-intervention won't work, but existing efforts may still be too slow and limited to arrest an emerging gap between U.S. goals and capabilities.

As I have testified elsewhere, at least some of the key military hardware requirements to meet these objectives are straightforward and affordable.[23] We must make particular effort to preserve the significant U.S. advantage in undersea warfare by emphasizing nuclear-powered attack submarines (SSNs) and offensive naval mines. We must also take a page from China's counter-intervention playbook and prioritize anti-ship cruise missiles (ASCMs). We are already facing a significant reduction in SSN numbers because of earlier decisions that are resulting in rapid retirement of *Los Angeles*-class SSNs without corresponding replacements to maintain force levels. That's why I have consistently emphasized the following bottom line: if we're not building at least two *Virginia*-class SSNs per year, we're not being serious—and regional allies, partners, and China will see that clearly. Three a year would be even better, and I believe we can and should get there soon.

Closing a True Missile Gap

We should never have allowed American ASCM development to languish so terribly. While I recognize and commend the important efforts underway now, I remain concerned and believe we need to move further, faster. Here's why:

Regardless of China's precise economic trajectory, China's navy—together with its other military and paramilitary forces—will be increasingly capable of contesting U.S. sea control within growing range rings extending beyond Beijing's unresolved island and maritime claims in the South China, East China, and Yellow Seas. Experts at the annual conference we convened at CMSI earlier this year generally agreed that by 2020, China is on course to deploy greater quantities of missiles with greater ranges than those systems that could be employed by the U.S. Navy against them. China is on track to have quantitative parity or better in surface-to-air missiles (SAMs) and ASCMs, parity in missile launch cells, and quantitative inferiority only in multi-mission land-attack cruise missiles (LACMs). Land-based missiles with potential to threaten U.S. ships and ports they deploy from include the world's only anti-ship ballistic missile—the numbers of which constitute only a tiny fraction of the world's foremost sub-strategic ballistic missile force deployed by China. Let me be clear: *Unless this gap can be filled credibly, China is poised to "outstick" the U.S. Navy by 2020 by deploying greater quantities of missiles with greater ranges than those of the U.S. ship-based systems able to defend against them.*[24]

Retention of U.S. Navy superiority hinges on next-generation long-range ASCMs (the Long-Range Anti-Ship Missile/LRASM and the vertical launch system-compatible Naval Strike Missile/NSM variant). These remain "paper missiles," as yet un-fielded on U.S. Navy surface combatants. The NSM represents the extraordinary case of the United States looking to Norway (in partnership with Raytheon) to supply a key weapons system that American industry itself should have been able to produce on favorable terms years ago. Additionally, new U.S. ASCMs may be unable to target effectively under contested A2/AD conditions. Failing to fill this gap would further imperil U.S. ability to generate and maintain sea control in the Western Pacific.

Let me underscore once again that the U.S. and China *can* avoid war. I'm confident that we *will* avoid fighting each other. Rather, this is about maintaining robust deterrence in peacetime and in any crises that might erupt. Specifically, we must deter Beijing from attempting to resolve island or maritime claims disputes with the use of force, or even the threat of force. The aforementioned weapons systems, effectively deployed and combined with a broader strategy, can repeatedly convince China's leaders that they will not succeed in their objective if they attempt to use military force to seize additional features and waters around them, or to prevent U.S. forces from operating in international waters and airspace nearby.

Maintaining Freedom of Navigation

Proper efforts in the abovementioned areas will thereby support access to pursue our vital interests, which include unfettered access to all areas of operation allowed by international law. This access is not only in the form of freedom of navigation *per se*, but also to support a much broader set of fundamentals: access for American military force, economic power, political persuasion, and influence over regional events. All require the support of military power that underwrites American influence on behalf of the global system.

Supporting freedom of navigation, in turn, requires a broad array of measures, coordinated through a whole-of-government approach. Freedom of navigation operations should be pursued proportionally, in accordance with international law, whereby islands and rocks are accorded territorial waters and airspace out to twelve nautical miles, and reefs (features naturally underwater at high tide) are accorded zero nautical miles. Such legal distinctions are important, and we should operate accordingly.

Additionally, we need to reinforce the global institutions that the Law of the Sea was designed to create and support. This entails underwriting with our power and example peaceful dispute resolution based on international law and international institutions. Among these, the United States must ratify the UN Convention on the Law of the Sea (UNCLOS). As Peter Dutton testified before the House Foreign Affairs Committee in 2014, "American policy makers must realize that the contest for East Asia is one of both power and law. ... Acceding to [UNLCOS] and once again exercising direct leadership over the development of its rules and norms is the first and most critical step. ... My sense is that East Asian states, indeed many states around the world, are desperate for active American leadership over the norms and laws that govern legitimate international action."[25] Once again, I agree fundamentally with my colleague.

Regaining Legal Leadership

The United States should ratify UNCLOS because doing so would further support the rules-and-norms-based international system that Washington is rightly trying to foster—in part as a means to ensure the following: (1) that neither force, nor even the threat of force, will be employed to resolve island and maritime claims disputes in a dynamic but increasingly-tense region; and (2) that such destabilizing approaches will not be encouraged anywhere else. Ratifying UNCLOS would also eliminate a perennial source of deflective criticism by China and understandable concern on the part of U.S. allies and partners. While the U.S. stance with regard to international maritime law is obviously far more sophisticated than this—including nuanced positions regarding the far-reaching applicability of customary international law—ratifying UNCLOS would nevertheless eliminate a perception that Washington is advocating "Do as I say, not as I do." The application of maritime law in practice is shaped over time, and China is already benefitting from U.S. vulnerability in this area—vulnerability caused by not joining 166 other nations in becoming a party to UNCLOS.

I can attest from personal experience to the extent to which China has cultivated a new generation of sharp, persistent maritime legal specialists who are active in the international arena. I believe that their concerted efforts can make a difference over time, a difference that would undermine the governance of the global maritime commons to our collective detriment.

But don't just take it from me. What's far more important is that UNCLOS ratification is supported by:

1. The current President, Secretary of State, Secretary of Defense, Chairman of the Joint Chiefs of Staff; and the heads of the U.S. Maritime Services: Navy, Marine Corps, and Coast Guard
2. All their living predecessors, from Republican and Democratic administrations alike[26]

On how many issues does one witness this sort of unanimity across parties, agencies, and time? These people are true experts: not just on theory, but on how things play out in policy practice. There is a compelling reason for their unanimity: U.S. UNCLOS ratification is a great idea whose time has more than come.

Worth Defending: Not Thucydides' World, But the Twenty-first Century Global System

Safeguarding the long-term future of the global maritime commons, including the freedom of the vital international sea-lanes of the South China Sea and the airspace above them, demands nothing less than the measures I have advocated here. We will have to accept some moderate friction, but we can *manage* that—all while cooperating with China and other nations in areas of mutual interest. We live in a far better world today than Thucydides could ever have dreamed of. Let's be sure to keep it that way in all respects, for everyone, regardless of their relative power.

Thank you very much for your attention.

[1] "Summary of the Position Paper of the Government of the People's Republic of China on the Matter of Jurisdiction in the South China Sea Arbitration Initiated by the Republic of the Philippines," Ministry of Foreign Affairs of the People's Republic of China, 7 December 2014, http://www.fmprc.gov.cn/mfa_eng/zxxx_662805/t1217149.shtml.

[2] *The PLA Navy: New Capabilities and Missions for the 21st Century* (Suitland, MD: Office of Naval Intelligence, 2015), 43, http://www.oni.navy.mil/Intelligence_Community/china_media/2015_PLA_NAVY_PUB_Interactive.pdf.

[3] 万启光 [Wan Qiguang], 南海水产公司志 [A Record of South China Sea Fisheries Company], (Beijing: 海洋出版社 [Ocean Press], 1991), 115-33.

[4] Andrew S. Erickson and Conor M. Kennedy, "Tanmen Militia: China's 'Maritime Rights Protection' Vanguard," *The National Interest*, 6 May 2015, http://www.nationalinterest.org/feature/tanmen-militia-china%E2%80%99s-maritime-rights-protection-vanguard-12816.

[5] Andrew S. Erickson and Conor M. Kennedy, "Meet the Chinese Maritime Militia Waging a 'People's War at Sea'," China Real Time Report (中国实时报), *Wall Street Journal*, 31 March 2015, http://blogs.wsj.com/chinarealtime/2015/03/31/meet-the-chinese-maritime-militia-waging-a-peoples-war-at-sea/.

[6] Daniel R. Russel, Assistant Secretary, Bureau of East Asian and Pacific Affairs, "Remarks at the Fifth Annual South China Sea Conference," The Center for Strategic and International Studies, Washington, DC, 21 July 2015, http://www.state.gov/p/eap/rls/rm/2015/07/245142.htm.

[7] For specific details, see "Island Tracker," Asia Maritime Transparency Initiative, Center for Strategic and International Studies, http://amti.csis.org/island-tracker/.

[8] As elsewhere in this testimony, italics are inserted by author for emphasis.

[9] For a detailed explanation, see Andrew S. Erickson, "Lengthening Chinese Airstrips May Pave Way for South China Sea ADIZ," *The National Interest*, 27 April 2015, http://nationalinterest.org/blog/the-buzz/lengthening-chinese-airstrips-may-pave-way-south-china-sea-12736.

[10] Peter A. Dutton, "Did the Game Just Change in the South China Sea? (And What Should the U.S. Do About It?)," *A ChinaFile Conversation*, 2 June 2015, http://www.chinafile.com/conversation/did-game-just-change-south-china-sea-and-what-should-us-do-about-it.

[11] Peter A. Dutton, Professor and Director, China Maritime Studies Institute, U.S. Naval War College, Testimony before the House Foreign Affairs Committee, Hearing on China's Maritime Disputes in the East and South China Seas, 14 January 2014, http://docs.house.gov/meetings/AS/AS28/20140114/101612/HHRG-113-AS28-Wstate-DuttonP-20140114.pdf.

[12] Peter A. Dutton, "Did the Game Just Change in the South China Sea? (And What Should the U.S. Do About It?)," *A ChinaFile Conversation*, 2 June 2015, http://www.chinafile.com/conversation/did-game-just-change-south-china-sea-and-what-should-us-do-about-it.

13 For a Chinese description of such a concept, see "张召忠: 反制菲占岛 只需用 '包心菜' 战略" [Zhang Zhaozhong: To Counter the Philippines' Encroachment on Islands, [We] Need Simply to Employ the "Cabbage" Strategy], 环球网 [Global Network], http://mil.huanqiu.com/observation/2013-05/3971149.html.

[14] Andrew S. Erickson, "Did the Game Just Change in the South China Sea? (And What Should the U.S. Do About It?)," A ChinaFile Conversation, 29 May 2015, http://www.chinafile.com/conversation/did-game-just-change-south-china-sea-and-what-should-us-do-about-it.

[15] China's paramount leader himself has declared that "We should work together to promote the democratization of international relations." ("我们应该共同推动国际关系民主化.") Xi Jinping, "习近平在和平共处五项原则发表 60 周年纪念大会上的讲话 (全 文)" [Speech of Xi Jinping on the Five Principles of Peaceful Coexistence at the 60th Anniversary Commemoration (Full Text)], Ministry of Foreign Affairs of the People's Republic of China, 28 June 2014, http://news.xinhuanet.com/politics/2014-

06/28/c_1111364206.htm. See also, "Full Text: China's Peaceful Development Road," *People's Daily*, 22 December 2005, http://english.peopledaily.com.cn/200512/22/eng20051222_230059.html.

[16] "The U.S. Alliance System and the Lack of True Multipolarity," in Thomas J. Christensen, *The China Challenge: Shaping the Choices of a Rising Power* (New York: W.W. Norton & Company, 2015), 49-52. See also Thomas J. Christensen, "China's Military Might: The Good News," *Japan Times*, 8 June 2015, http://www.japantimes.co.jp/opinion/2015/06/08/commentary/world-commentary/chinas-military-might-the-good-news/#.VXcGOM9VhBc; Thomas J. Christensen, "Managing Disputes with China," *Japan Times*, 9 June 2015, http://www.japantimes.co.jp/opinion/2015/06/09/commentary/japan-commentary/managing-disputes-china/#.VXcDYEaDRBy.

[17] Andrew S. Erickson, "Assessing the New U.S. Maritime Strategy: A Window into Chinese Thinking," *Naval War College Review* 61.4 (Fall 2008): 35-71, http://www.usnwc.edu/getattachment/21380430-28cf-4a54-afbb-cb1f64761b27/Assessing-the-New-U-S--Maritime-Strategy--A-Window.aspx.

[18] "Remarks by President Obama and President Xi Jinping of the People's Republic of China After Bilateral Meeting," White House, 8 June 2013, http://www.whitehouse.gov/the-press-office/2013/06/08/remarks-president-obama-and-president-xi-jinping-peoples-republic-china-.

[19] Shi Yinhong, "An Analysis of the 'New-Type of Major-Country Relationship,'" *China-US Focus*, 3 April 2014, http://www.chinausfocus.com/print/?id=36897.

[20] "Chapter 2: This Time Should Be Different: China's Rise in a Globalized World," in Thomas J. Christensen, *The China Challenge: Shaping the Choices of a Rising Power* (New York: W.W. Norton & Company, 2015), 37-62.

[21] This has been more recently termed "New-Type Major Country Relations," but without any apparent change in its underlying meaning.

[22] For detailed analysis, see Andrew S. Erickson and Adam P. Liff, "Not-So-Empty Talk: The Danger of China's 'New Type of Great-Power Relations' Slogan," *Foreign Affairs*, 9 October 2014, https://www.foreignaffairs.com/articles/china/2014-10-09/not-so-empty-talk.

[23] Andrew S. Erickson, "China's Naval Modernization: Implications and Recommendations," Testimony before the House Armed Services Committee Seapower and Projection Forces Subcommittee, "U.S. Asia-Pacific Strategic Considerations Related to PLA Naval Forces" hearing, Washington, DC, 11 December 2013, http://docs.house.gov/meetings/AS/AS28/20131211/101579/HHRG-113-AS28-Wstate-EricksonA-20131211.pdf.

[24] Andrew S. Erickson, Personal summary of discussion at "China's Naval Shipbuilding: Progress and Challenges," conference held by China Maritime Studies Institute at U.S. Naval War College, Newport, RI, 19-20 May 2015, http://www.andrewerickson.com/2015/07/quick-look-report-on-cmsi-conference-chinas-naval-shipbuilding-progress-and-challenges/.

[25] Peter A. Dutton, Professor and Director, China Maritime Studies Institute, U.S. Naval War College, Testimony before the House Foreign Affairs Committee, Hearing on China's Maritime Disputes in the East and South China Seas, 14 January 2014, http://docs.house.gov/meetings/AS/AS28/20140114/101612/HHRG-113-AS28-Wstate-DuttonP-20140114.pdf.

[26] See, for example, Adm. Bob Papp, Commandant of the U.S. Coast Guard, "Benefits of joining the Law of the Sea Convention," *The Hill*, 19 April 2012, http://thehill.com/blogs/congress-blog/foreign-policy/222647-benefits-of-joining-the-law-of-the-sea-convention; John B. Bellinger III, Adjunct Senior Fellow for International and National Security Law, "Should the United States Ratify the UN Law of the Sea?" *Council on Foreign Relations*, 11 November 2014, http://www.cfr.org/treaties-and-agreements/should-united-states-ratify-un-law-sea/p31828.

Mr. PERRY. Thank you, Dr. Erickson.

Now turn to Dr. Rapp-Hooper for her testimony.

STATEMENT OF MIRA RAPP–HOOPER, PH.D., FELLOW, ASIA PROGRAM, DIRECTOR, ASIA MARITIME TRANSPARENCY INITIATIVE, CENTER FOR STRATEGIC & INTERNATIONAL STUDIES

Ms. RAPP-HOOPER. Chairman Perry, Congressman Bera, I am honored to have this opportunity to discuss regional states' responses to China's recent activities in the South China Sea. My testimony today will summarize my written statement and will focus primarily on responses by countries that have sovereignty claims and occupy territory, including the Philippines, Vietnam, Malaysia, and Taiwan. I will argue that there are ample opportunities for the United States to advance its interest in the South China Sea in tandem with other regional states.

As Ranking Member Sherman noted, land reclamation and construction did not begin with China's building efforts in 2014. South China Sea claimants began to set up outposts in the Spratly Islands in the 1950s, and several have undertaken major island renovations since that time. The Philippines, Vietnam, Malaysia, and Taiwan all do have airstrips of their own on Spratly outposts, and all have stationed troops on these islands at some point in time.

When these other claimants are compared to China, however, the size, scope, and speed of their building activities absolutely pales in comparison. To paraphrase Secretary of Defense Carter, China has gone farther and faster in its construction activities, and this first chart that you see up on the screen will help you visualize the amount of land that each country has reclaimed.

By way of comparison, Taiwan has reclaimed approximately 5 acres over 2 years, Malaysia reclaimed approximately 60 acres over 30 years, Vietnam 50 to 60 acres over 5 years, whereas China has reclaimed at least 2,000 acres over 1 year at seven different locations.

Since China's widespread land reclamation activities have become known, other claimants have responded with some modest construction activities of their own. More significant, however, are the visible diplomatic and military shifts that have taken place in the region over the last 18 months.

Claimant states have sought naval and Coast Guard capabilities with clear South China Sea applications. These include Coast Guard patrol vessels, transport ships, corvettes, landing crafts, anti-submarine warfare helicopters, submarines, and patrol aircraft. Claimant states have also commenced training exercises with new partner militaries and drills that are explicitly focused on defense in the maritime domain.

In the past year, the Philippines, Vietnam, and Malaysia have all pursued new strategic partnerships in the region. Most obviously, an alliance is emerging between Manila and Hanoi, but claimants have all forged ties amongst themselves and also with India, Japan, and Australia. These patterns leave little doubt that other claimants hope to counteract China's assertiveness in the South China Sea, but this will be no easy feat.

After two decades after annual double-digit increases in its defense spending, China's military budget is six times larger than Southeast Asia's, and its capabilities overwhelm those of other regional states. As this next chart demonstrates, China's Navy and Coast Guard outnumber those of all the other claimants when combined.

Many regional states also see an interest in maintaining positive relationships with China. Several of the South China sea claimants are likely to participate in China's Maritime Silk Road Initiative. Washington cannot assume that opposing sovereignty claims will always beget strictly opposing policies and strategies.

Regional states share many of the United States' South China Sea concerns, but they are neither unambivalent, nor monolithic in their opposition, nor do their worries necessarily translate into coordinated policy responses. Washington must, therefore, take these variegated inclinations into account as it advances its interests alongside those of regional partners.

First, the United States should insist that all claimants refrain from any major physical changes or militarization of the territories they presently occupy. In recent weeks, China has turned to publicizing Vietnam's land reclamation and construction activities. And while these absolutely pale in comparison to Beijing's, this building still feeds China's narrative that it is playing a defense game of catch-up, and this gives it convenient talking points in domestic as well as international fora.

The United States should also define a criteria for what constitutes militarization as opposed to civilian use of an island. And these photos you will see up on the screen give you some sense of the extent of Chinese land reclamation on both Fiery Cross and Mischief Reef on the left, compared to Vietnamese reclamation and additions to Sand Cay on the right.

Second, the Pentagon's $425 million Southeast Asia Reassurance Fund may provide some much-needed support to the coast guards and navies of other South China Sea claimants. Partner capacity-building efforts, however, are long-term initiatives that will take years to bear fruit, and some states will have trouble absorbing assistance officiently and effectively. Washington should establish a mechanism to coordinate partner capacity-building efforts with Australia, Japan, and India, so that the support may be mutually reinforcing.

Dr. Cronin already mentioned a number of ways the United States can work with ASEAN to share more information, so I will conclude my remarks today by emphasizing the importance of the United States collecting and publicizing data on freedom of navigation and overflight risks. Multiple countries, including the United States, have already been warned away from China's artificial islands, which are not entitled to national airspace or to territorial waters if they were not islands when construction began.

These incidents should be well documented, shared amongst the relevant parties, and periodically publicized, because this data is crucial to any judgment about whether U.S. and regional states' interests are being imperiled by China's activities. By taking these steps, Washington can maximize regional buy-in for its policies and advance its South China Sea interests in tandem with other states.

Multilateral approaches alone are unlikely to arrest China's incremental opportunism. They can, however, help to coalescence some much-needed regional consensus in the South China Sea.

Thank you.

[The prepared statement of Ms. Rapp-Hooper follows:]

CSIS | CENTER FOR STRATEGIC & INTERNATIONAL STUDIES

Statement before the House Committee on Foreign Affairs Subcommittee on Asia and the Pacific

"AMERICA'S SECURITY ROLE IN THE SOUTH CHINA SEA"

A Statement by:

Dr. Mira Rapp-Hooper

Director, Asia Maritime Transparency Initiative,
Center for Strategic and International Studies (CSIS)

July 23, 2015

2172 Rayburn House Office Building

WWW.CSIS.ORG   1616 RHODE ISLAND AVENUE NW | TEL: (202) 887.0200
WASHINGTON, DC 20036 | FAX (202) 775.3199

Chairman Salmon, Ranking Member Sherman, distinguished members of the Subcommittee, I am honored to have this opportunity to discuss regional states' responses to China's recent activities in the South China Sea. My testimony today will focus primarily on responses by countries that have sovereignty claims and occupy territory in the South China Sea, including the Philippines, Vietnam, Malaysia, and Taiwan. I will also address noteworthy responses by Japan, Australia, India, and regional institutions.

Regional states share many of the United States' interests in the South China Sea, including freedom of navigation and overflight, the peaceful resolution of disputes, and upholding international law. Claimant state actions are also motivated by their national sovereignty claims, which, as a neutral party, the United States does not necessarily share. I will argue that there are, however, ample opportunities for the United States to advance its interests in the South China Sea in tandem with those of other regional actors. To that end, I will conclude my testimony today by offering some suggestions on how the United States can use multilateral mechanisms to enhance security in this vital waterway.

Land Reclamation and Construction History in the Spratly Islands

Land reclamation and construction in the South China Sea did not begin with China's building efforts in 2014. South China Sea claimants began to set up outposts in the Spratly Islands in the 1950s, and several have undertaken land reclamation and construction efforts since that time. Malaysia occupies five Spratly features and reclaimed land and constructed facilities on Swallow Reef in 1983. The Philippines occupies eight features and has constructed facilities. Taiwan occupies one feature. It has reclaimed a small amount of land and is currently in the midst of airstrip and port renovations. Vietnam, which occupies as many as 29 features, has reclaimed land and built military and civilian facilities. Vietnam, Philippines, Malaysia and Taiwan all have airstrips of their own on Spratly outposts, and all four have stationed troops on these islands.

When these other claimants activities are compared to China's in size, scope, and speed, however, their building activity pales in comparison. To paraphrase Secretary of Defense Carter, China has gone farther and faster in its construction activities. The breakneck pace and widespread use of land reclamation and construction, rather than the mere fact of the building itself is what raises serious concerns about China's intentions in the Spratlys for other South China Sea claimants. It is also worth noting that China is the only country to have completely transformed features that were formerly under water into artificial islands; other countries have used the technique to add some additional acreage onto features that were already above water.

By way of comparison, Taiwan has reclaimed approximately five acres of new land over two years at one location. Malaysia reclaimed approximately 60 acres over 30 years at one location. Vietnam reclaimed 50-60 acres over five years at one location. China, however, has reclaimed at least 2,000 acres over one year at seven different locations.

For many countries in the region, the timing of these building activities is also significant. In 2002, China and ASEAN signed a Declaration on Conduct in the South China Sea. This agreement commits the parties to "exercise self-restraint in the conduct of activities that would complicate or escalate disputes and affect peace and stability..." in the area. The Declaration does not expressly prevent building on features that are already occupied, but many claimants feel that China has violated the spirit of the document with its recent activities, and that these activities have made it much less likely that the claimants will be able to negotiate a long-sought, binding Code of Conduct for the South China Sea.

Construction Responses to China's Activities
Since China's widespread reclamation activities became known in mid-2014, other claimants have responded with construction of their own. In the last few years, Vietnam has engaged in a small amount of additional land reclamation and added new facilities to two of its islands. In early 2015, Malaysia announced that it would install an air defense system on Swallow Reef. Taiwan's modest use of land reclamation has occurred over the course of the last year, and is part of a renovation that will upgrade its airfield and build sophisticated port facilities. After announcing a moratorium in construction activities in 2014, the Philippines decided in March of this year that it would repair and renovate its military facilities on Thitu Island. It is also reinforcing the hull of a ship that it uses as a military outpost in the Second Thomas Shoal.

Balancing Behavior by South China Sea Claimants

More significant than claimants' construction responses are the visible diplomatic and military shifts that have taken place in the region in the last 18 months. Regional states have sought new military capabilities, increased the frequency and pursued new types of military exercises, and advanced new political partnerships within the region.

New Military Capabilities
Since early 2014, South China Sea claimant states have invested heavily in the purchase of new military capabilities, most of which have clear maritime applications. Some of these investments were part of ongoing military modernization programs and cannot be solely attributed to China's recent assertiveness in the Spratlys, but there is little doubt that claimant states are focusing their acquisitions on defense in the maritime domain.

The Philippines has announced a 15-year force modernization plan that includes plans to procure fast attack craft, stealth frigates, anti-submarine warfare (ASW) helicopters, and submarines. Manila will purchase from Tokyo 10 patrol vessels for its coast guard, and has received a patrol corvette and transport ship from South Korea, two landing crafts from Australia, and two strategic sealift vessels from Indonesia. It will purchase fighter aircraft from South Korea, and will receive a total of five C-130 Hercules transport aircraft from the United States. It has decided to expand a major naval base at Oyster Inlet on the South China Sea side of Palawan Island, and just last week announced that it will begin stationing a full squadron of new FA-50 aircraft and two naval frigates at the former U.S. naval facility at Subic Bay. The Philippines Air Force has also decided to grant to the United States access to two Philippine bases that will allow for rapid ingress to the South China Sea.

Vietnam is seeking maritime patrol boats and aircraft, unarmed drones, and fighter jets. Its navy and coast guard are receiving patrol ships from Japan and from India. It has purchased 3rd generation Kilo-class submarines as well as land-attack and anti-ship missiles from Russia. It has also been reported that Vietnam would like to purchase P-3 patrol aircraft from the United States.

Taiwan has announced that it will develop eight diesel-electric submarines indigenously beginning in 2016. In June, it commissioned two coast guard patrol vessels capable of docking at Itu Aba Island in the South China Sea. Taiwan is purchasing four guided missile frigates from the United States, as well as four additional P-3 Orion patrol aircraft that were part of a 2007 deal.

In October 2014, Malaysia announced a 10% increase in its defense budget, including a six percent increase in procurement and research. It will purchase six corvettes from France, and has announced that it will purchase additional corvettes, six anti-submarine warfare helicopters, other small vessels, and will replace torpedo and missile systems.

It is worth noting, however, that with the exception of Taiwan, the other South China Sea claimants have scant naval and coast guard capabilities. Their recent investments are clear indicators of their concern, but will not offset China's vast military advantages.

Exercises
As tensions have risen in the region, South China Sea claimant states have added new training exercises to aid in their defensive preparations. These have included exercises with new partner militaries, as well as novel drills that are explicitly focused on defense in the maritime domain.

The Philippines has been eager to exercise near the South China Sea and with new partners. The 2014 bilateral U.S.-Philippines Cooperation Afloat Readiness and Training (CARAT) exercise was held 80 miles from Scarborough Shoal and included live fire drills and amphibious operations. The Philippines sent vessels and personnel to the Kakdu international maritime exercise in Australia, and received Australian personnel and aircraft for the U.S.-Philippines Balikatan exercise. The Philippines and Japan held their first-ever combined naval exercise in May 2015. In June 2015, The Philippines and Japan held another exercise which included a P-3 overflight of the disputed Reed Bank in the South China Sea.

In August 2014, Vietnam held new exercises with India near its coast. The United States has conducted six consecutive years of non-combat Naval Engagement Activities with the Vietnamese military, including medicine and search and rescue operations.

In 2014, Taiwan's navy and marines simulated a simultaneous retaking of Itu Aba in Taiwan's largest South China Sea drill since 2000. This was also the first time a Taiwan

South China Sea drill included regular troops as opposed to coast guard personnel. In April 2015, Taiwan's Ministry of National Defense reported that it would begin to dispatch P-3 Orion maritime patrol aircraft on anti-submarine reconnaissance and surveillance missions beyond Taiwan's Air Defense Identification Zone (ADIZ) and into the South China Sea.

The United States and Malaysia have held new military exercises, including a new bilateral amphibious exercise, a U.S. Marine Corps demonstration, and their annual Cooperation Afloat Readiness and Training (CARAT) joint bilateral exercise. In May 2015, Malaysia and the United States conducted a major bilateral exercise in the South China Sea that included a U.S. carrier strike group.

Emerging Political Partnerships
China's assertiveness has also encouraged new diplomatic and political relationships. In 2014-2015, the Philippines, Vietnam, and Malaysia have all pursued new strategic partnerships.

The Philippines has established a strategic partnership with Vietnam, which will pave the way for more joint drills, information sharing, and training. Manila has also had public support from India in its pursuit of an international legal recourse for South China Sea disputes. The Philippines and Japan are also contemplating a Visiting Forces Agreement (VFA) that would allow Japanese aircraft and naval vessels to access Philippine bases on a rotational basis.

Beyond its strategic partnership with the Philippines, Vietnam has sought several new political relationships. Vietnam and Japan have established a strategic partnership to promote military-to-military cooperation and capacity building. Vietnam and India released a joint statement pledging defense cooperation and mutual interests in the South China Sea. Hanoi has also pushed to upgrade its defense ties with Indonesia to improve bilateral training and exchanges. Vietnam and Australia have agreed to establish a strategic partnership in the future, with an emphasis on security cooperation, training, and the South China Sea. The United States and Vietnam have agreed to deepen military cooperation in areas such as humanitarian assistance and disaster relief (HA/DR) and search and rescue (SAR). Finally, in July 2015, General Secretary Trong became the first Vietnamese Communist Party Chief to visit the United States. His joint vision statement with President Obama expressed support for freedom of navigation, international law, and rejected the use of coercion. The two leaders also agreed to increase coordination on maritime security and maritime domain awareness.

In 2014-2015, Malaysia and Indonesia took steps towards settling their territorial disputes and improving bilateral relations. Malaysia and Japan penned a new strategic partnership in May 2015, and this will include coast guard capacity building as well as the possibility of defense equipment and technology transfers. In April 2014, Malaysia hosted President Obama for the first visit by a U.S. president in 50 years, and the two countries have upgraded their relationship to a comprehensive partnership.

These defense procurement patterns, exercises, and nascent partnerships leave little doubt that other claimants are seeking to balance China's assertiveness in the South China Sea. This will, however, be no easy feat. After two decades of annual double-digit increases in its defense spending, China's military budget is six times larger than all of Southeast Asia's and its military capabilities overwhelm those of other regional states. China's navy and coast guard outnumber those of all of the other claimants combined. As China continues to invest in its military and lay down new hulls at breakneck speed, claimants have sought assistance from other partners in the region. In 2014-2015, they have begun to find it in Japan, Australia, and India.

Balancing by other U.S. Allies

Japan

China's land reclamation campaign has unfolded as Japan is undertaking a historic overhaul of its national security policy. This has allowed Tokyo to pursue new strategic partnerships and exercises with the Philippines, Vietnam, and Malaysia. The leadership in Tokyo has also been outspoken in its objections to China's Spratly construction activities. Japanese officials, including Prime Minister Shinzo Abe, have consistently reaffirmed Japan's commitment to freedom of navigation, respect for international law, and the peaceful resolution of disputes in the region.

Since early 2015 there has also been frequent public discussion about the possibility of Japan participating in aerial patrols of the South China Sea. Some reports have suggested that Tokyo and Washington may conduct joint patrols, that Japan may conduct patrols alongside other claimants, or that it may conduct surveillance and reconnaissance operations on its own. There are, however, important operational, fiscal, and domestic political impediments to Japanese South China Sea patrols. At present, Japan does not have aircraft available to devote to a South China Sea mission, nor does it have adequate refueling capabilities to conduct them. Japan's defense budget has traditionally been set at around one percent of GDP, and five year spending caps prevent Tokyo from deviating materially from this target. Finally, the Abe government is currently in the midst of advancing national security legislation that will allow it to take a more active defense role in the region, but these bills have met with more domestic backlash than anticipated. Japan's interest in patrols should certainly be taken as an indicator of its deep concern for the security and stability of the South China Sea, but the obstacles that may prevent it from assuming a near-term leadership role cannot be discounted.

Australia

Australia's foreign and defense ministers have been outspoken in their opposition to China's land reclamation and militarization of its South China Sea outposts. Top officials in Canberra have also made clear that they would oppose any efforts by China to interfere with freedom of navigation or overflight in the South China Sea, and would contest an Air Defense Identification Zone (ADIZ). The Australian government has also reportedly considered conducting a freedom of navigation exercise near China's artificial islands. Australia has held two recent military exercises with the Philippines, and donated vessels to Manila. It has also signed comprehensive partnership with Hanoi, which may be upgraded to a strategic partnership in the future.

India

Indian Prime Minister Narendra Modi has announced and begun to implement an "Act East Policy" to bolster Delhi's ties with the region. At the 2014 India-ASEAN and East Asia Summits, Indian officials emphasized freedom of navigation, the peaceful resolution of disputes, and the importance of international law. In September 2014, India and Vietnam issued a joint communique opposing threats to freedom of navigation and the use of coercion in the South China Sea. In September 2014 and January 2015, Modi and President Obama released joint statements that affirmed common interests in the South China Sea. In June 2015, India and the United States signed a defense framework that includes a pledge to "increase each other's capability to secure [...] freedom of navigation across sea lines of communication." In June 2015, India also sent a four-ship naval flotilla to Malaysia, Singapore, Indonesia, and Australia, as part of a visit to the South China Sea.

Multilateral Responses

Countries in the region have also reacted to China's assertiveness through multilateral mechanisms. In its April 2015 Chairman's Statement under the leadership of Malaysia, ASEAN expressed serious concern about China's land reclamation activities, stating that they had "eroded trust and confidence and may undermine peace, security, and stability in the South China Sea." The statement reaffirmed ASEAN states' interest in freedom of navigation and overflight and urged that consultations towards a South China Sea Code of Conduct be expedited. While not transformative, these were stronger and more unified statements than many experts expected.

In an early June Senior Officials Consultation (the 21st of its kind), China and ASEAN pledged to conclude a Code of Conduct. In early July, China and ASEAN held a Joint Working Group meeting. The group identified some Code of Conduct elements for "early harvest," including programs on navigation safety and search and rescue. It is worth noting, however, that many officials and analysts remain pessimistic that China and ASEAN will conclude a South China Sea Code of Conduct in the foreseeable future.

Outside of ASEAN, interested parties are considering multilateralizing their relationships to more effectively engage Chinese challenges in the South China Sea. The Philippines, Brunei, Indonesia, and Malaysia have discussed the possibility of signing a Status of Visiting Forces Agreement that would allow the nations to train together. The VFA would provide temporary base access for each country in the Philippines. Reportedly, Vietnam, India, and Japan have privately agreed to work in a trilateral format to coordinate security policies. U.S. Pacific Fleet Commander Admiral Scott Swift has also suggested expanding longstanding bilateral combat exercises with allies and partners in the region into multi-nation drills focused on the South China Sea.

Bandwagoning Behavior

Despite these multifaceted efforts to counteract China's assertiveness, regional states have not sought exclusively to balance Beijing. Many see an interest in maintaining positive strategic relationships with China, including on security issues and the South China Sea disputes. In October 2014, Vietnam and China pledged to repair their ties and better manage their maritime and territorial disputes in a high-profile agreement. Malaysia and China held their first-ever bilateral military exercise, entitled "Peace and Friendship," in December 2014.

Perhaps the most complex political relationship among the South China Sea claimants is that between Taiwan and China. Despite the many unsettled issues that define Cross-Strait relations, Taiwan and China share South China Sea claims, as embodied by China's Nine-Dash and Taiwan's Eleven-Dash Line. U.S. government officials have urged Taiwan to clarify or abandon its opaque claim line, but it has declined to do so. In 2014, Taipei criticized Vietnam's presence at Sand Cay in the Spratly Islands as dangerous and destabilizing. More recently, as the International Tribunal on the Law of the Sea began South China Sea hearings at The Hague in July, Taiwan made public statements that appeared to align with China in its rejection of the court's jurisdiction.

Several of the South China Sea claimants are likely to participate in China's Maritime Silk Road initiative and may be the recipients of infrastructure aid, participate in China's Trans-Asia Railway, and are likely to continue to boost bilateral trade ties.

Even if claimant states do not explicitly align themselves with China, their desire to maintain positive relations with Beijing may mean that they do not engage in unequivocal balancing behavior. When it comes to regional states' responses to China in the South China Sea, Washington cannot assume that opposing sovereignty claims will always beget strictly opposing policies and strategies.

Recommendations for U.S. Regional Engagement

The last fifteen months of regional reactions to China's island building indicate that the claimants share many of the United States' interests in and concerns about the safety and security of the South China Sea. They are, however, neither unambivalent nor monolithic in their opposition to Beijing's activities, and their deeply-held worries do not necessarily translate into a coordinated policy response. Washington must take these variegated inclinations into account as it pursues policies to foster maritime security and regional stability. There are several steps that the United States can take that will help to advance its interests in the South China Sea alongside regional partners and allies:

1) **Halt to All Land Reclamation and Militarization:** At the 2015 Shangri-La Dialogue, Secretary of Defense Carter called for an end to land reclamation, not just by China, but by all claimants. China's Spratly land reclamation activities are now nearly complete, but as its building has continued to receive international scrutiny, it has turned to publicizing Vietnam's land reclamation and construction activities. Vietnam's activities pale in comparison to China's. The fact that it has reclaimed any land and installed new military equipment, however, feeds China's narrative that it is playing a defensive game of catchup and gives Beijing

convenient talking points in domestic and international fora. The United States should insist that all claimants refrain from any major physical changes to or militarization of the territories they presently occupy.

2) **Coordinate Partner Capacity Building:** The Pentagon's $425 million Southeast Asia Reassurance Fund may provide much-needed support to the coast guards and navies of other South China Sea claimants. Partner capacity building efforts are long term initiatives that will take years to bear fruit, and the United States is *not* the only country giving this type of aid. Some regional navies and coast guards will have trouble absorbing assistance efficiently and effectively. Washington should establish a mechanism to coordinate partner capacity building efforts in Southeast Asia with Australia, Japan, and India, so that training and equipment support is mutually reinforcing.

3) **Maritime Domain Awareness:** Maritime Domain Awareness (MDA) capabilities for Southeast Asia should top Washington's list of partner capacity building priorities. The United States should help to fund a multilateral monitoring architecture that can help claimants develop a common picture of the South China Sea. China's construction developments on its artificial islands may proceed in fits and starts over the coming months, but other claimants will be better able to coordinate their responses if they are not taken by surprise by developments and are working from the same set of facts.

4) **ASEAN Briefings:** Before this MDA network is up and running, the United States should use ASEAN as a forum through which to share information about China's island facilities. Briefings should be given at ASEAN Regional Forum (ARF) and ASEAN Defense Ministerial (ADMM-Plus) meetings, so that regional states understand the nature and implications of China's island projects as Beijing develops them and have more opportunities to coordinate responses.

5) **ASEAN Code of Conduct:** U.S. policymakers should continue to call for a Code of Conduct for managing the South China Sea disputes, but should encourage ASEAN states to draft a document themselves and then offer China the opportunity to accede to it. Because ASEAN-China negotiations have no time limit and are based on consensus, China has been able to slow-roll this process while incrementally revising the territorial status quo in its favor.

6) **Freedom of Navigation and Overflight Risk Assessments:** Numerous U.S. partners have reaffirmed their commitment to freedom of navigation and overflight, and some have stated that they would firmly oppose a South China Sea Air Defense Identification Zone if China announced one. Less publicized, however, is the fact that multiple countries, including the United States, have already been warned away from China's artificial islands, which are not entitled to national airspace or territorial waters if they were not islands when construction began. These incidents should be well-documented, shared among relevant parties, and periodically publicized. This data is crucial to any judgment about whether U.S. and regional states' interests are imperiled by China's activities, and will inform subsequent action in the region.

By taking these steps, Washington can maximize regional buy-in for its policies and advance its South China Sea interests in tandem with other states. Multilateral approaches alone are unlikely to arrest China's incremental opportunism, which began well before its recent dredging activities. They can, however, help to coalesce much-needed regional consensus in the South China Sea.

―――――――

Mr. PERRY. Thank you, Dr. Rapp-Hooper.

We now recognize Dr. Swaine for his testimony.

STATEMENT OF MICHAEL D. SWAINE, PH.D., SENIOR ASSOCIATE, ASIA PROGRAM, CARNEGIE ENDOWMENT FOR INTERNATIONAL PEACE

Mr. SWAINE. Thank you, Mr. Chairman. It is a pleasure to be invited to testify here today. Since I have only got 5 minutes, I will focus on what I think U.S. interests are in the South China Sea, and what I think the United States should do under the current situation there.

In my view, the USG's message on the South China Sea has been badly garbled, making it seem as if Washington is opposed to any Chinese activities that involve an increase in presence or capability in the area with little serious reference to the actions of anyone else. There is definitely a dynamic going on here. It is not just China's behavior.

The U.S. needs to focus like a laser on its two only really vital interests in the South China Sea that it should be prepared to act to support via words and action. First is freedom of navigation and concerns that China might eventually use its growing position, including land reclamation, to attempt to interdict the activities of the U.S. Navy in the open ocean.

This is not about commercial obstruction. The Chinese have absolutely no interest in obstructing commercial transit in the South China Sea and emphasizing this issue is distracting and doesn't serve the interests of the United States. This is about the access of the U.S. Navy and other military navies into the area.

The second issue and the second interest of the United States is a possible use of force against other claimants that can produce a much greater level of tension and push the region toward an emphasis on security over economic growth. Now, both of these interests involve potential violations over disputes regarding international law and process, including three issues, whether man-made islands can be used to create 12 nautical mile territorial seas and EEZs, whether a coastal state with EEZs can demand that foreign militaries notify them before transiting or engaging in ISR activities, and of course the resort to force over disputed territories.

Now, these issues have existed for a long time in U.S.-China relations. The U.S. and China have somewhat different views on some of these issues, but the South China Sea problem, combined with China's growing capacity to influence the area, raises their salience. The reason for concern over the form issue, freedom of navigation, derives primarily from China's lack of clarity in defining the nature of its maritime claims within the Nine-Dash Line and its rejection of the U.S. position on EEZs, on the use of foreign militaries in EEZs.

The reason for concern over the latter interest, which is a use of force derived from the fact that: A) China has employed force in the past to eject other claimants from disputed South China Sea territory; and b) China and others seem to offer little strong support at present for adopting a binding code of conduct in the South China Sea. Not just China, but ASEAN countries as well are having real trouble bringing that about.

So what should the United States do? In the remaining time, let me just tick off seven points. The first, I think the U.S. Government needs to significantly tone down its repeated very public protests regarding land reclamation, and focus instead on expressing the reasons why it is concerned about the two interests I enumerated above.

Land reclamation in itself is meaningless. Virtually every claimant has engaged in it, and to say that China is doing more of it means very little. Moreover, Washington can't induce Beijing to stop it, if it were to start again, absent a larger stabilization process to which all parties agree. The issue is not the reclamation; the issue is what China is doing with the land that it is reclaiming.

Second, Washington should stop emphasizing military deterrence methods to prevent changes in the status quo, thus freezing a situation into one of constant potential conflict, and start focusing instead on the resolution of territorial disputes through negotiations between the claimants designed to clarify the nature of claims, first of all.

All the different claimants have different claims, and they are having agreement on what those claims consist of. This should be followed by the application of UNCLOS principles to sort out the territorial and EEZ implications of the claims, perhaps using something like a South China Sea Council modeled after the Arctic Council, to try and disentangle these claims.

Third, at the same time, Washington also needs to make it clear privately to Beijing that its continued failure to enter into such talks on these issues, and to clarify the nature of its claims to waters within the Nine-Dash Line, combined with its growing presence and capabilities in the area, will increasingly cause the U.S. and other states to draw worst-case conclusions and act accordingly to hedge against such outcomes.

So the U.S. would need to maintain its own capacity and the capacity of others to counter possible future attempts by Beijing to declare a de facto exclusionary zone, or zones in the area, or to employ force possibly against an ally such as the Philippines.

Washington should make it clear, fourth, that such hedging would require a significant improvement in U.S. defense relations in presence with Manila, as well as Hanoi and Malaysia. But this augmented activity should be made contingent on China clarifying its claims and entering into negotiated codes of conduct with significant progress with the other claimants.

Beijing must also clearly affirm, in my view, through its words and actions, that there is no military solution to these disputes and that we will never seek to dislodge rivals forcefully from occupied areas. Washington should make it clear that if China undertakes such actions and pledges, the U.S. would suspend the above hedging activities.

Fifth and sixth, regarding negotiations, Washington should stop opposing bilateral talks between claimants, including China-Vietnam, China-Philippines, et cetera, and try to broker bilateral settlements between Vietnam and the Philippines and Vietnam and Malaysia, so as to reduce the differences among the Southeast Asian claimants at the bilateral level with China. That would give them more leverage in their dealings with China. The U.S. needs to really support that process.

Sixth, in order to reduce tensions and improve the environment for negotiations, Washington should work behind the scenes to organize an effort to promote the joint exploration of seabed resources without prejudice to sovereignty, as has already been done by several bilateral states in the region.

And then, finally, while Japan's efforts to improve the capability of Coast Guard units of our allies and friends in Southeast Asia is welcomed, Washington should not encourage the Japanese self-defense force to join the U.S. in patrolling the South China Sea. Having the joint self-defense force in the South China Sea where Japan has no territorial claims, and its security and freedom of navigation are not threatened, would intensify the emerging security dilemma between the U.S.-Japan alliance and China and promote instability.

Thank you very much.

[The prepared statement of Mr. Swaine follows:]

CARNEGIE
ENDOWMENT FOR
INTERNATIONAL PEACE

Congressional Testimony

America's Security Role in the South China Sea

Testimony by **Michael D. Swaine**
Senior Associate, Asia Program
Carnegie Endowment for International Peace

Testimony before the House Foreign Affairs
Subcommittee on Asia and the Pacific

July 23, 2015

Thank you for inviting me to testify today.

For the United States, the South China Sea is an important area of the Asia-Pacific region for three reasons: 1) it is part of a major transit route for maritime commercial traffic to and from East Asia and for the U.S. Navy; 2) disputes over the ownership of its many small islands, reefs, atolls, and rocks among China and several nearby Southeast Asian states (including one U.S. ally, the Philippines) are generating tensions that could result in conflict and instability; and 3) Beijing could eventually use its growing influence in the area to create a sphere of influence detrimental to U.S. interests.

These factors justify U.S. attention to events occurring in the South China Sea, and a set of policies designed to ensure access and transit, prevent or minimize tensions, and support the peaceful and legally based management of local disputes. Unfortunately, U.S. statements and actions at present are not effectively achieving such objectives, and growing tensions over the issue are threatening to severely destabilize the critical U.S.-China relationship in unnecessary ways.

Reacting to continued Chinese land reclamation efforts on several reefs in the Spratly Islands, senior U.S. officials and military officers vow to "fight tonight" if needed to defend U.S. interests across the Indo-Pacific, while referring to Chinese claims across the South China Sea as "preposterous" and Chinese land activities there as designed to "militarize" the region and to build a "great wall of sand." In response, Chinese officials and spokespersons warn the U.S. against provocative actions, insist that China will not back down and reiterate their determination to "safeguard our own sovereignty and territorial integrity."

Meanwhile, this heated rhetoric is being fueled by all manner of often misleading claims, charges, and demands for more aggressive action by outside commentators on both sides. Many in the U.S. see China as engaged in a concerted strategic effort to seize control over the entire South China Sea, land and water alike, as part of a larger attempt to push the U.S. out of Asia and replace it as the dominant force in the region. Only a more aggressive and sustained military-centered U.S. pushback designed to deter and humble China will avert this outcome, they insist.

In contrast, many in China see the U.S. as using the disputes over sovereignty in the South China Sea and elsewhere as a means of justifying more concerted efforts to contain and undermine all Chinese influence in the Asia-Pacific, and to encourage other states to provoke China and militarize the issue. Beijing must double its efforts to strengthen its position and show the U.S. and others that China cannot be intimidated, they demand.

This situation is not just another temporary downward blip in an up and down Sino-U.S. relationship. It threatens to drive U.S.-China relations in a far more adversarial, zero-sum direction and destabilize the region. To allow a dispute over a few rocks and islands in a corner of the Asia-Pacific region to derail a vital relationship critical to both regional and global peace and prosperity is the height of folly. Hyperbolic statements, veiled threats and calls for more military action serve no useful purpose and will only lead to hardened positions and redoubled efforts on both sides to counter the other. What is needed is a far sharper level of clarity by both Beijing and Washington regarding their claims, grievances and concerns, and, on that basis, a clear indication of the consequences of unacceptable behavior, along with a commitment to provide mutual assurances over the near term to avoid specific tripwires, while working to stabilize the long term situation.

Washington's message on the South China Sea issue has been badly garbled, making it seem as if it is opposed to any Chinese activities that involve an increase in presence or capability in the area, with little serious reference to the provocative actions of any other claimants, in particular Vietnam and the Philippines. To clarify its position, the U.S. needs to focus like a laser on its two only real interests in the South China Sea, and connect its statements and actions to them as much as possible.

The first interest is freedom of navigation (FON), meaning access **by the U.S. Navy** to areas outside any legally established territorial waters surrounding islands or other features, including the so-called Exclusive Economic Zone (EEZ) that extends for 200 nautical miles beyond such waters. China has no interest in obstructing commercial shipping or flights across the South China Sea and warning them against something they have never undertaken and would never do in the future, except perhaps in time of war, is unnecessarily provocative and misleading.

The second U.S. interest regarding this issue is the possible unprovoked use of force by China against other claimants. Such actions would inevitably generate a much greater level of tension across the region and push it toward an emphasis on military rivalry over peaceful economic growth. Both Washington and Beijing have a vital interest in preventing an escalating spiral of violence over disputed rocks and islands. Washington needs to end its vague opposition to undefined "coercion" by Beijing or others in the South China Sea and focus on preventing the sustained use of force.

Both of these U.S. interests involve potential violations of or disputes regarding international law and process in respect to three issues: 1) whether man-made islands can be used to justify 12nm territorial seas and EEZs that can then be used to limit naval access; 2) whether a coastal state with EEZs can demand that foreign militaries notify them before transiting or engaging in ISR or similar military activities; and 3) the threat or resort to force over disputed territories.

Regarding the first point, the U.S. must make it abundantly clear to the Chinese government that any attempt to claim sovereign waters or EEZs for man-made islands built on features that do not possess territorial waters or EEZs would be in violation of international law and completely unacceptable. Washington has in fact said this at times, but too often it also makes statements that give the impression that it is opposed to Chinese land reclamation per se. Land reclamation in itself is meaningless. Virtually every claimant has engaged in it, and to say that China is doing more of it means little. The issue is about what China **does** with its reclaimed land.

In addition, the lack of Chinese clarity regarding the specific claim to waters around man-made islands is magnified by its larger unwillingness to clearly define its claims to those waters existing *outside* of any conceivable 12 nm limit or EEZ associated with land features and yet *inside* the much larger "nine-dashed line" (9DL) that is intended to signify its claims across the South China Sea. Beijing has at times acted as if it has exclusive rights over such waters, but has never clearly stated its position, thus greatly increasing the overall level of uncertainty. Washington and others have repeatedly called for Beijing to clarify its stance on the 9DL and should continue to do so.

On the second point (regarding naval activities within EEZs) Beijing and Washington clearly differ over how freely U.S. military assets can operate in areas just outside territorial waters, especially the EEZ. China, along with several other coastal nations such as India and Brazil, insists that it has the legal right, under the regulations of the UN Convention on the Law of the Sea (UNCLOS), to deny foreign navies the ability to conduct a variety of supposedly "hostile" activities in its EEZ, including surveillance. The U.S. and many other countries reject this interpretation. Moreover, China has itself conducted such supposedly "hostile" naval actions (i.e., surveillance) in the U.S. EEZs around Guam and Hawaii. Washington must point out the hypocrisy of the Chinese position and insist that it has a right to operate in a non-hostile manner (including normal surveillance activities) outside of legal 12 nm territorial waters. At the same time, Washington should reduce the frequency of its monitoring activities within China's EEZs. It is my understanding, based on discussions with former U.S. officials, that the U.S. military does not need to conduct such ISR activities at high levels.

The third point (an unprovoked threat or use of force) would constitute a clear violation of the UN Charter prohibiting such behavior. Any sustained attempt by China to forcibly threaten or remove other claimants from disputed territories without any clear appeal to self-defense would seriously disrupt peace and generate a strong regional and international response. Beijing must recognize that such an outcome would undermine its entire "peaceful development" policy and put at risk its relations with the West and many regional states. Although China has stated many times that it is committed to a peaceful process of negotiation over the disputed areas and signed the 2002 *Declaration on the Conduct of Parties in the South China Sea*---in which all parties agreed "to resolve their territorial and jurisdictional disputes by peaceful means, without resorting to the threat or use of force,"---it has never clearly disavowed an unprovoked use of force. Moreover, China has employed force in the past to eject other claimants from disputed South China Sea territories, and at present it (along with many ASEAN states) seems to offer little strong support for adopting a binding Code of Conduct to avoid future incidents. The U.S. and others should thus press China and other claimants to make a clear, definitive statement that they will not resort to force to remove other claimants without a direct, prior provocation. Some might counter that China and others could not make such a pledge without damaging its sovereignty claims in the South China Sea or undermining its future negotiating leverage. However, such consequences are avoidable if Beijing makes its non-use-of force- pledge contingent on similar pledges by other claimants and defines its pledge clearly as a confidence building measure that in no way imperils its sovereignty claims.

In addition to the above near-term actions in support of its two interests in the South China Sea, Washington should also undertake several specific actions to prevent the further deterioration of the situation over the long term. First. Washington should stop emphasizing military deterrence methods to prevent changes in the status quo (thus freezing the situation into one of constant potential conflict) and start focusing instead on the resolution of territorial disputes through negotiations between the claimants designed to clarify the nature of claims. This should be followed by the application of UNCLOS principles to sort out the territorial and EEZ implications of the claims, perhaps using South China Sea Council modeled on the Arctic Council.

Second, Washington needs to make it clear privately to Beijing that its continued failure to enter into binding Code of Conduct talks, to clarify the nature of its claims to waters within the 9DL, and to disavow the unprovoked use of force, combined with its growing presence and capabilities in the area, will increasingly cause the U.S. and other states to hedge against worst case outcomes and act accordingly. Specifically, the U.S. will need to maintain its own capacity, and the capacity of others, to counter possible future attempts by Beijing to declare a *de facto* exclusionary zone or zones in the area and to employ force, possibly against an ally (the Philippines).

Third, Washington should make it clear to Beijing that such hedging would require a significant improvement in U.S. defense relations and presence with, and the provision of armaments to Manila, as well as Hanoi and Malaysia. However, this augmented level of U.S. activity should *be made contingent on* China clarifying its claims and entering into negotiated codes of conduct with other claimants. Beijing must also clearly affirm, through its words and actions, that there is no military solution to these disputes and that it will never seek to dislodge rivals forcefully from occupied areas in an unprovoked manner. It should also refrain from deploying significant power projection capabilities on its occupied islands in the Spratly Islands, such as advanced fighters. Washington should make it clear that, if China undertakes such actions and pledges, the U.S. *would suspend* the above hedging activities, but would restart them if China violates its commitment.

Fourth, regarding negotiations over the disputed claims, Washington should stop opposing bilateral talks between claimants, including China-Vietnam, China-Philippines and China-Malaysia, and try to broker bilateral settlements between Vietnam and the Philippines and Vietnam and Malaysia so as to reduce differences between claimants to the bilateral level with China. The current U.S. stance of pushing "collaborative" efforts is a non-starter in the absence of any unity among the non-China claimants.

Fifth, in order to reduce tensions and improve the environment for negotiations, Washington should work behind the scenes (perhaps with Indonesia) to organize an effort to promote the joint exploration of seabed resources without prejudice to sovereignty, as has already been done by Malaysia and Thailand (1979), Malaysia and Vietnam (1992), and Malaysia and Brunei (2009), and as China has long urged. Washington should call Beijing's apparent bluff on this issue.

Sixth while Japan's effort to improve the capacity of coast guard units of our allies and friends in Southeast Asia is welcome, Washington should not encourage the Japan Self-Defense Force to join the U.S. in patrolling the South China Sea. Having the JSDF in the South China Sea where Japan has no territorial claims (unlike China) and its security and freedom of navigation are not threatened would intensify the emerging security dilemma between the US-Japan alliance and China and promote instability. Moreover, it is highly likely that Japan is legally prohibited from engaging in such joint patrols.

Finally, this issue, and the need for greater clarity regarding concerns and consequences, is sufficiently urgent and important to justify discussion at the highest levels of government. It should be on the agenda of President Xi Jinping's meeting with President Obama during the former's upcoming state visit to Washington in September. Rather than yet again exchanging each side's formal position, the two presidents and their aides should seek to achieve a clearer and more finely grained understanding of concerns, intentions, and consequences and commit themselves to undertaking mutual assurances designed to avoid an escalating spiral. Military and civilian authorities at lower levels could then develop such assurances.

The U.S. and China must get beyond the heated rhetoric and signals of resolve and build the basis for demilitarizing and defusing the escalating tensions in the South China Sea. If this is not done, the current course of action threatens to produce a far more dangerous situation that will prove extremely difficult to reverse.

Thank you.

Mr. PERRY. All right. Thank you, ladies and gentlemen, for your testimony.

I will begin with questions. And, let me see, I think I am going to go—I think I will actually start with you, Dr. Swaine. And some of this is going to be—quite honestly, I think you have gone through because, you know, you are here to kind of describe the situation but also offer some remedy that each of you have as I have listened and taken notes.

But if you could, some of you say, you know, "Congress needs to do this." And we can get into the whys and the why nots, but I think the administration also bears some responsibility to do some things as well. So if you could, maybe codify like your top three things, right, and so we can—I would hope that this subcommittee would be instrumental in forming legislation to further our efforts and our interests in that regard.

So with that, in light of China's aggressive land reclamation over the past 18 months, many argue that the United States should support its allies and partners in the region through economic and military assistance. Others say that the Southeast Asia nations must take ownership of their own ongoing disputes with China.

So the question is: How should the United States navigate the correct balance between supporting our partner yet reducing risks of dependence and overreliance on the United States? Dr. Swaine.

Mr. SWAINE. Well, as I mentioned in my remarks, I think—I mean, it is a difficult challenge to strike this balance correctly, but I think the balance needs to be placed on Chinese actions and expectations of Chinese behavior and what the United States is prepared to do if there isn't a clarification of the Chinese position.

As I said in my testimony, I don't think the United States should preemptively begin building up the capabilities of other countries in the area, regardless virtually of what China is doing, as a kind of insurance policy.

Mr. PERRY. Okay.

Mr. SWAINE. I think it needs to link what it is going to do in that regard of any significance with certain expectations about China's clarification of its behavior.

Mr. PERRY. Dr. Rapp-Hooper.

Ms. RAPP-HOOPER. Thank you, sir. I think it is an excellent question, but I would just add on and clarify the fact that risks can exist on both sides of the ledger. So when we are considering the prospect of giving additional aid to partners in Southeast Asia—for example, the Philippines—to build up their naval and coast guard capabilities, we are envisioning a process that will take certainly years to bear fruit, as I mentioned in my testimony.

But by improving the Philippines' Coast Guard capability, we improve the ability of the Philippines to engage in these issues by itself and——

Mr. PERRY. So you are not advocating for a mutually exclusive kind of policy where we would engage the Philippines in that regard at the disregard of China. I would assume you are talking about both simultaneously.

Ms. RAPP-HOOPER. Absolutely. And it is worth noting that because the United States of course does have a treaty guarantee to the Philippines that if the Philippines, with its very modest naval and coast guard capability were to be pulled into conflict, this engages U.S. commitments and credibility. So there is some U.S. interest in considering the capabilities of the Southeast Asian partners.

Mr. PERRY. Dr. Erickson.

Mr. ERICKSON. I want to echo Dr. Rapp-Hooper's recommendations regarding building partner capacity. That is extremely important. I also fully believe that our deterrence relationship with China is both manageable and important, and we need to maintain it by consistently funding and keeping on track the weapon systems that I mentioned in my testimony and that I am happy to elaborate on further.

The two other things I would recommend very strongly are to continue to pursue access through our freedom of navigation operations pursued proportionately in accordance with international law. So based on what specific features enjoy on based on widely recognized international legal principles. That is how we should operate close to those features, regardless of what China says, regardless of what China does. That is international law.

Mr. PERRY. So if I may interject at this moment, have we attempted that? And have we been stopped or thwarted in that?

Mr. ERICKSON. To the best of my knowledge—and my research involves solely unclassified sources, so I recommend getting full briefings on all of this—I think we have succeeded thus far in our freedom of navigation operations. I think it was valuable to have that publicized on CNN, and I believe what was publicized was an example of something that we do frequently in international waters and airspace around the world, and that we should continue to do.

If I may, Mr. Chairman, let me emphasize one other very strong policy recommendation that I think is extremely important. My colleagues here have emphasized the importance of international law access, freedom of navigation, and to me this is part of supporting the larger system that we have all described here, and that I believe that you and Mr. Bera have also rightly emphasized in terms of this system that we need to support.

And we need to support it both with our power and our example, and that is why I think it is critically important that we join 166 other nations in finally ratifying the U.N. Convention on the Law of the Sea, to take that excuse off the table that China has to bludgeon us with even though in a very nuanced and sophisticated fashion we adhere to customary international law.

And, in closing, let me just emphasize, this is not something that you have to take from me. I far more recommend that you listen to this recommendation from the current President, Secretary of State, Secretary of Defense, Chairman of the Joint Chiefs of Staff, Heads of the U.S. Maritime Services—Navy, Marine Corps, Coast Guard—and all of their living predecessors, from Republican and Democratic administrations alike. So please allow me to underscore that point.

Thank you.

Mr. PERRY. Thank you. I appreciate it.

Dr. Cronin.

Mr. CRONIN. Well, Mr. Chairman, to reiterate my remarks, we need to leverage and build our comprehensive power, economically in terms of new development initiatives to show that we bring solutions to the region that really matter. Politically, we need to be more engaged. I talked about engaging ASEAN on four different levels. We need to build our diplomatic and our legal means.

But we have to also leverage our power. If we are going to shape this region, which is being shaped every day by China's rise and China's opportunism, we are going to have to leverage our power. And we need to do that, including on the military side, by two basic types of building partnership capacity.

One of them is just sharing information, transparency, what Dr. Rapp-Hooper does for a living every day, sharing the facts and getting them out there as we saw in these pictures, but also we need to build partnership capacity, not because this antagonizes China but because a minimal credible deterrent in defense goes a long way toward raising the bar toward aggression and toward assertiveness, unilaterally changing the facts on the ground. So we need to do that.

We also, though—and one recommendation I had for the administration, but really for Congress to basically insist, was go ahead and ask for a comprehensive interagency approach to, how do you impose costs on bad behavior? And I do believe the administration needs to be more clear about what exactly constitutes the kind of unacceptable behavior, because I do agree with Dr. Swaine we have been too general about this issue.

We do need to be clear about what exactly—let us narrow down the set of issues that we think basically violate UNCLOS and international law and the rules, as well as the declaration of conduct that ASEAN and China agreed to in 2002, and what is really just part of growing, what is just part of the development of the region. We do need to narrow down that set, because we don't object to everything.

Just the opposite. Effective cooperation with China is very important. We need to insist on qualitative improvement in the relations—effective MOUs on avoiding incidents at sea and in the air, insisting that the summit meeting include a very serious discussion about intentions in the South China Sea.

Mr. PERRY. Thank you to the panel.

At this point, I will recognize Mr. Bera.

Mr. BERA. Thank you, Mr. Chairman.

You know, just listening to the witnesses, we all have the same goal, which is de-escalate tensions and the real goal of avoiding military confrontation, which is not the goal here.

You know, if I contrast it, just thinking about what—China's unilateral moves and the East China Sea expanding their air defense identification zone, and what our response, the U.S. along with Japan, in not recognizing this and actually, you know, conducting preplanned operations over that air. That was a proportionately strong response, that, you know, in many ways while the tension still exists, the tensions in the South China Sea seem very much more acute.

I agree with Dr. Cronin that we have to operate from a position of strength in the United States, you know, and that is not, you know, with our military, but it is trying to engage these rules of maritime law and coming up with rules of maritime law, so there are mechanisms of dispute resolution.

It is also empowering I think, again, as each of you mentioned, and I think specifically Dr. Cronin, empowering China and the 10 ASEAN nations to come to terms with what these rules look like, and come to terms with, you know, there will continually be disputes that arise over maritime territories. But we have to have mechanisms by which to de-escalate and resolve these.

You know, maybe starting with Dr. Cronin, if you want to talk to what it would take to get China and the ASEAN nations to agree to what these maritime rules are and what our role could be to continue pushing this forward.

Mr. CRONIN. Nobody I know who is involved in looking at this prolonged code of conduct being negotiated between China and the 10 ASEAN states—it has now dragged on since the 2002 declaration of conduct of the parties of the South China Sea—believes that this is going anywhere quickly. Even the Chinese dismissed the idea that this could be readily resolved.

We need to work on multiple tracks. I don't think we need to wait for China. We can encourage the claimant states. We can encourage ASEAN. We can encourage the claimant states and parts of ASEAN, plus outside countries like India, Australia, and Japan, to go ahead and say, ''This is a voluntary code of conduct.'' These are basically the ways of behavior that we will expect, the upholding of UNCLOS, essentially the principles—and I have enumerated them in my full written testimony, 12 different points of law.

It is not just what Dr. Swaine; there are points of baseline law. There are lots of points of law that are being run roughshod over, as Dr. Erickson said, that we need to help reinforce. And I think we can agree among a key coalition of countries, starting with the claimant states, and we have been pushing and helping and facilitating. We can provide more facilitation, by the way.

This is a foreign affairs issue, legal, political facilitation and help to not only allies like the Philippines but partners like Vietnam, working with Malaysia, Brunei, the four claimant states of ASEAN, in terms of helping them to think through how to come to terms with the rule of law.

Mr. BERA. And is it your sense that if we were to engage in let us say a voluntary code of conduct, and invite the claimant states to engage, would most of those be willing to participate in this conversation, outside of China?

Mr. CRONIN. Well, we know that the Philippines and Vietnam are at the leading edge of this concern and interest. They are both interested, and I think there is an opportunity there. I think Malaysia is extremely interested, but they have always played it very carefully because they have the largest trading relationship of any ASEAN country with China. Mixed with that, they have their own political turmoil going on at the moment.

Brunei will essentially probably follow Malaysia. So I think there is an opening there. I think we can make this happen.

Mr. BERA. And a goal of this is not to be anti-China. A goal of this is to establish norms of trade, norms of maritime law, norms of airspace law.

Mr. CRONIN. Yes, sir.

Mr. BERA. Again, from my perspective, it is not to be anti-China. It is to establish these norms of commerce.

Mr. CRONIN. Mr. Bera, I think you are exactly right. That is exactly what we want. We want rules that we can all live by. These are rules, after all, that China has thrived by in many ways since opening up at the end of the 1970s. We want to establish those rules and adapt them and evolve them for all. We are not trying to be unfair, and we have to be very careful to be fair, but we do want rules we can all live by.

Mr. BERA. And if these—and maybe Dr. Erickson or Dr. Rapp-Hooper, if these voluntary conversations are moving forward and the ASEAN nations are participating, is your thought that China eventually would, you know, join this conversation? Whoever wants to take that.

Mr. ERICKSON. That's an excellent question. I think the conversation can be complex in some ways in terms of how China will participate. But what we really need here is for everyone to live by the same rules, regardless of what conversation they have. These rules and norms are not a mystery. They already exist.

What we need to do is make sure that they are enforced and that everyone has the confidence and the security that this is how the system works. And that is why our power and example can help, including through partnership building capacity. These are sovereign states, some allies, which have a fundamental right to their own military and paramilitary, coast guard capabilities.

We do not want to encourage the creation of a world in which only big countries get to pursue those things, and the small ones just have to cower and accept whatever comes. That is not the world we want to see, nor is it the world we have to accept.

Mr. BERA. And we are in the final stages of negotiating a very significant trade deal with many of these claimant nations. It would seem to me that part of this trade deal, as we set the rules of commerce in the Asian Pacific, would provide us an opportunity, an opening by which to also address some of these. Would that be an accurate, you know——

Mr. ERICKSON. Just allow me to quickly say I could not agree more. TPA and TPP are a critical, constructive, mutually profitable part of this. And I think that without productively pursuing those avenues we simply can't have a multi-faceted Asia Pacific policy and presence that underwrites all of these other interests that we have outlined today. I couldn't agree more strongly.

Ms. RAPP-HOOPER. Just to tack on to Dr. Erickson's comment, many of our friends and partners in the region see TPP as a national security issue. They see it not only as a trade deal but as a sign of the U.S.'s commitment to the region, an enduring commitment to the region. Even countries that are not negotiating partners in this round of TPP are urging us to pass this deal, because they do see it as much more than just a trade deal itself.

Mr. SWAINE. If I could just comment on the issue of working with the other countries in the region, as I said in my testimony, I think it is very important for the United States to really begin focusing more on the reasons why the ASEAN states themselves have not been able to really achieve much in the way of a consensus in how they look at the problem of the South China Sea.

I mean, some people would tell you that the main obstacle to a code of conduct is not china. It is the fact that the Southeast Asian states themselves have no agreement among themselves. Vietnam and Malaysia, Vietnam and the Philippines, they have enormous disputes about what their claims consist of, what a code of conduct should look like, all of those issues.

So on that basis, then, it is almost impossible to have a collaborative, as Hillary Clinton said at one time, approach to dealing with this issue. That is not going to happen. Unless the Southeast Asian countries themselves gain more agreement about how this issue—what the meaning of this issue is and how to proceed with it, you are not going to see much in the way of coordinated action toward the Chinese, and I would dare say you are not going to see a whole lot of movement on the part of the Chinese. So I think that sort of emphasis and the degree to which the United States can facilitate it is important.

Now, on the other hand, the United States needs to be aware of the fact that the more it becomes deeply engaged and involved in the efforts in a high visibility way the more difficult it is going to be to achieve an objective. And the reason for that is because Southeast Asian states on their side look to the United States to do a lot of the heavy lifting. And that takes the burden off of them, so they don't have to be quite as responsible in moving forward and making certain concessions, because they think the United States might be backing them.

Secondly, it makes the Chinese more defensive, because they think, ah, the United States is really creating all of this behind the scenes, or in front, and that is in their view the primary obstacle to reaching any kind of understanding is because of U.S. involvement in the issue.

Now, you don't have to accept their Chinese argument by any means. I am just telling you the dynamic, though, is such that calculations on both sides, Chinese and Southeast Asian, are such that U.S. involvement could not—would not necessarily in every case be a facilitator. And anybody who is involved in this has to be very sensitive to that.

Mr. BERA. I yield back.

Mr. PERRY. Thank you.

The acting Chair now recognizes the chair of the subcommittee, Mr. Salmon, the gentleman from Arizona.

Mr. SALMON. Thanks a lot. Appreciate you all coming today. This is such an important issue, not just to our country but to many of our allies in the region as well.

I am going to ask you to speculate a little bit. Maybe it will be based on knowledge. Maybe it will be based on, I don't know, supposition. But what do you really think that at the end of the day China's motives are in doing this island building? What are their intentions for placing offensive armaments on these islets? Do you think that there is any serious concern about that? Or do you think that they are just trying to find natural resources that are valuable? What do you think that they are after?

Dr. Cronin, do you want to start? Yes.

Mr. CRONIN. Chairman Salmon, thank you very much for your leadership and the excellent question. It is supposition. We don't know. We don't know. My speculation is that there is a great deal of opportunism going on right now. China is making it up as they go along.

But this is driven by very long-standing claims and new-found capabilities and opportunity. And we are giving them more opportunity than they ought to have as they rewrite the rules and create the facts on the ground. So the Nine-Dash Line, which isn't based on contemporary and international law, needs to be held to a point of law.

What are they doing with arms on these artificial islands? They are partly intimidating the neighbors. They are partly declaring their seriousness of intent to these claims. They are staking out administrative control. They are trying to preempt international legal proceedings, in my view, in terms of the Philippine arbitration case next year that may come to fruition.

They will have already built, as we have seen by Dr. Rapp-Hooper's statistics, 2,000 acres added on to these roofs. And adding arms that Dr. Erickson talked about allows them to say, ''Look, we are not only administering; we control these. These are de facto ours. We are not moving, and that is our intent.'' It is about regional order and about respect from their perspective. It is about claiming their role in the region of the world.

But capabilities matter, intentions may change, so these intentions right now which may be, even if they are very defensive and even if they are very much driven by history and a fear of what the others have done, it is not fair that others started to build runways before they built a runway. I can understand the need for nationalism on the part of China. And we are trying to damp-down this nationalism, and I don't think fortifying these artificial islands with military arms is helping, which is why Dr. Rapp-Hooper is talking about trying to hold the line on new armaments going out there.

But, unfortunately, if China does go down the road of building up its military, building up its coast guard, building these forward staged artificial islands as bases, that they will create new capabilities still in terms of the ability to project power beyond what we often refer to as the first island chain out to the second island chain.

Now, they may have no serious intent in the political center right now on that. Those are certainly those in the PLA who think about it. But just because you are in the military and you think grand thoughts doesn't necessarily make it policy. So we don't know what their long-term intentions are, but we have to keep up with the day-to-day capabilities.

We need to be more engaged. I take Dr. Swaine's point that engagement is a double-edged sword, and we have to be very careful about America's role, especially in Southeast Asia. I have argued elsewhere that we can't go faster than the Southeast Asians in terms of trying to facilitate peace.

But at the same time, America has to be engaged every day in Southeast Asia. If I look out to the mid-century point of this century, Southeast Asia continues to grow. Indonesia goes prospectively to become the ninth largest economy, to the fourth largest economy in the world in this period of time. This is a very vital set of global waterways and economies that we are engaging. We need to be engaged for our own benefit and our future.

Mr. SALMON. I think you have answered a large part of what my next question was going to be, but there have been some that have asserted that this really isn't America's interest, that it is just a bunch of meaningless rocks and sand, and it is nothing that we should be too concerned about. What would you say to that?

Mr. CRONIN. My opening line, sir, before you arrived was that this is not most about rocks, reefs, and resources. It is about rules and order. But for us, for the United States, it is about opportunity. It is about the opportunity to continue to spread freedom and commerce that are at the root of the American republic from our founding.

We started to trade with Asia very early after our founding. We are going to have to stay engaged with the most dynamic economies of this world, which are in the Indo-Pacific. The latest IMF report shows what region is growing faster than any other? No surprise, Asia Pacific. What has grown faster since 1980? Asia Pacific. What is going to continue to grow faster than other regions, according to PricewaterhouseCoopers' latest forecast for 2050? Asia Pacific.

So if the United States wants to get on the bandwagon with the future of this global economy and stay strong and prosperous and free, we must be more engaged, and that includes the economies and the people of Southeast Asia already three—well, two-thirds of 1 billion people, but it is going to go up. Already $4 trillion in purchasing power parity of GDP. That is supposed to go way up between now and the next few decades.

This is vital for us. That is why things like the Trans-Pacific Partnership is a vital stepping stone to immediately second round talking to everybody, including to try to reconcile the different systems that are being built in global trading. Everything is changing. We have to be part of it, shape it, benefit from it, and bring our values and interests to this region.

Mr. SALMON. Dr. Rapp-Hooper, you made a comment about TPP. And I am sorry if I am paraphrasing, but it happens to coincide with my deeply held beliefs that TPP is far more than a trade agreement.

And what I see, a lot of our allies in the region believe—and having visited with them and talked with them as well—is that they worry that with a big void of American leadership in the region different rules, whether they are rules of the road for maritime space, whether they are rules of the road for trade, military engagement, different rules of the road will be crafted, and they will be crafted by others than the United States, and maybe it won't end up being a very pretty picture at the end. Do you have any thoughts on that?

Ms. RAPP-HOOPER. Mr. Chairman, I think that characterization is very apt. As I mentioned, I think a number of our allies and partners, including those who are not necessarily negotiating partners in this round of TPP, feel very strongly that this is a metric of American engagement and interest in the region over the long haul and see it as symbolically very important as a national security issue, not just as a trade deal.

I would also like to add some brief additions to Dr. Cronin's comments on the use of these islands, why China might be building up these islands. I think his assessment is absolutely correct. I would note that China, without these islands, did not before necessarily have the ability to engage in long-term, long-standing patrols in the southern parts of the South China Sea.

It has a limited resupply and refueling capability. So having an air base on Fiery Cross Reef, possibly having a second air base on Subi Reef, which may be coming in the next several months, gives it the ability to sustain more of a presence in the South China Sea. And, again, that goes to Dr. Cronin's point about the ambiguous Nine-Dash Line claim and China's ability to hold on to that claim.

These islands would theoretically be quite vulnerable in the case of an actual conflict, but they do potentially give China the ability to assert its claims in peacetime. And this gets to the essential question that you asked as to what America's interests are when it comes to the South China Sea.

I agree with Dr. Swaine that the United States should absolutely focus its rhetoric on a few items, which include freedom of navigation and overflight. Absolutely essential. And the fact that disputes should not be resolved using coercion, and this is absolutely what is at stake with this island building and the possibility of greater Chinese assertiveness from the islands.

Mr. SALMON. That having been said, what kind of a grade would you give our response or our leadership in the region on these kinds of issues? How are we doing? And any of you. Dr. Swaine, you wanted to make a comment. How do you think we are doing?

Mr. SWAINE. Well, it depends on what aspect of the policy and the objectives you are looking at, but I would say overall we are kind of at a B, B-minus. I think there has been very poor message discipline from the U.S. Government. There has been statements made by U.S. officials that I think have not been vetted, that have been unnecessary, in some ways inflammatory, have given the wrong impression about what U.S. policy is.

I think there needs to be more discipline in doing that. I think there also needs to be greater clarity. As I said in my statement, there needs to be greater clarity in exactly what the United States is objecting to.

ADIZs, on their own, are unobjectionable. The United has very large ADIZs. Japan has a very large ADIZ. The Chinese establishing an ADIZ, in and of itself, is not or should not be objectionable. It is about why they do it, when they do it, and how they use it. The same thing, as I just said, with land reclamation. The same thing with their presence in the South China Sea.

It is not the fact that they are there. They are going to be there. The fact is, what are they going to do with their presence? And if the Chinese are not clear enough about the basis of their claims to these areas and these waters, which has implications for how they then act, then it is a very difficult thing to determine exactly what is the best policy.

And as I said in my statement, the United States will be more inclined to have to hedge. And worst case, I think it is highly unlikely the Chinese are going to launch a military offensive to seize the entire Spratly Islands by force, ejecting all of the other claimants from their positions. By the way, the Vietnamese have the majority position in the South China Sea, in the Spratlys.

I think it is highly unlikely that they would do that. I think that their objective is much more, A, they feel they don't have enough leverage in the area. They feel they have been catching up. And I think to some degree—I mean, that is the Chinese position, but to some degree I think it is true. And they have tried to catch up their position there.

But, B, I think they see that their presence is a bigger presence, ultimately. They are going to have more capability, ultimately. And they want to establish a set of incentives, both positive and negative, and by ''positive'' I mean economic incentives and other positive things they can offer the other claimants, and ''negative'' in the sense of strong deterrent capability that will allow them to eventually make some kind of a deal.

Again, not based on force, not based on military invasion, but they want to be able to have the predominant position in the area, so that they can have some kind of negotiated settlement that would be to their advantage. I would say that is their ideal. They hope that they could get that. Now, in the meantime, I think they can exist with the current occupation of the areas, but the question is, under what conditions going forward? And I think that is a lot of what the diplomacy consists of.

Mr. SALMON. Thank you.

Anybody else want to comment?

Mr. CRONIN. Yes. Mr. Chairman, thank you for the leadership and focus that you are bringing to this vital region. It is tremendously important. Allow me to share my brief personal assessment of what I think are some of the challenges we have run into in our policy over the last few years, some areas in which we haven't performed the way we need to to further our interests and to support the global system in this vital region.

In the early years of the current administration, as made more difficult of course by the global financial crisis, I do think some unfortunate mistakes were made in terms of messaging, especially in optics, but words and optics matter. And we appear to be playing into Chinese rhetoric that made us look weaker and more distracted than would be effective in galvanizing allied and partnership support in the region, as well as maintaining a robust and stable deterrence relationship with China.

Two particular things. Some people dismiss these as just words, but I think these were a genuine mistake. First of all, several U.S. policymakers invoked an academic concept that China's paramount leader Xi Jinping himself invoked, a so-called Thucydides trap. This idea that based on previous history, if the rising power China and the existing power of the U.S. didn't make heroic efforts, do something very different, we couldn't avoid what would otherwise be an inescapable historical pattern of ruinous conflict.

I think that way of thinking is terribly misinformed. If you compare 1914 and 2014 plus, I think you can only argue that we are susceptible to the same type of historic risks if you don't believe in the transformative power of nuclear weapons, international institutions, financial markets, transnational production chains. These are all part of the global system many—or positive parts of the global system that we now all benefit from and that we should seek to defend.

So by appearing to agree with some of this rhetoric that was supported by China's own leader, we appear to be willing to yield to China's principle positions, and thereby contributed to emboldening Beijing to push back, to push harder, to probe, to see what China could achieve.

If you look at really decades, but including in recent years with high fidelity on various incidents, there is a pattern of China's leaders acutely attuned to their perception of changes in—even small changes in relative power and policy, and probing anew whenever they think there might be a change there. So we made that worse by appearing to embrace that rhetoric.

On a related note, we also made it worse by appearing to associate ourselves with what Chinese leaders initially rolled out as a new type of great power relations. This, too, appeared, although not fully defined, and we shouldn't have appeared to sign on to something that we didn't clearly have defined. But there is ample evidence to suggest that China's leadership, again, saw this as a way of saying that the U.S. had to yield to certain Chinese core interests in order to avoid a conflict in this new era.

So words matter. We initially did not do a good job with that. We have done much better with that, but we are still not fully out of the words on that, and we are paying the price for that to some extent.

Mr. SALMON. Thank you.

Mr. PERRY. Dr. Swaine?

Mr. SALMON. I think we are out of time, but go——

Mr. PERRY. I actually have another question.

Mr. SALMON. Okay. Well, go ahead. And if you want to comment, then please go ahead.

Mr. PERRY. Just to let the panelists know, I think we are expecting votes anytime. So as long as me and the chairman want to go back and forth and you are willing to stay here, we could run it to the end.

Moving to a little bit of a different topic, and I don't know your familiarity, but China has announced its China Sea air defense zone in 2013. Is the U.S. prepared for a scenario in which China announces a second ADIZ over parts of the South China Sea? And what would the likely U.S. response to such an action? I would start with Dr. Erickson, if you don't mind.

Mr. ERICKSON. Thank you very much for that extremely pertinent question, Mr. Perry. I think there is a very good chance that within the next 2 years that will no longer be an abstract question. Fortunately, I think the U.S. Government is very much on track to address this issue, because the solution in my view is to continue to pursue freedom of navigation and operate everywhere that is necessary for us in accordance with established, widely recognized principles of international law.

I think we have all seen the footage from the P–8 Poseidon aircraft that embarked—wisely embarked—a CNN reporter. We are already doing what we need to do in the event of China's declaration of an ADIZ over some parts of the South China Sea, namely treat it for what it is. It is in no way territorial airspace, and it is only relevant in terms of the coastal state issuing instructions to aircraft, if there is evidence that those aircraft intend to enter China's actual territorial airspace.

I agree with Dr. Swaine earlier. There is no rule against China establishing an ADIZ, and perhaps some of the U.S. messaging on that was a little bit garbled. I think we could do better. It was the way in which they rolled out the East China Sea ADIZ: China's military used the phrase, ''Defensive emergency measures'' would be used if aircraft entering this zone declined to comply with Chinese demands.

Well, that is simply against the basic principles of international law, and I would note that China has never conclusively taken back, walked back, those very inflammatory and destabilizing words. So if China—if and when China—announces an ADIZ over the South China Sea, the U.S., in my view, is going to be prepared to continue what we have already done—freedom of navigation.

And I don't believe that China is going to challenge that in a disruptive way, and I think we can all continue to go about business as usual. But that is what it is going to take.

Mr. PERRY. Oh, boy. Okay. Dr. Rapp-Hooper?

Ms. RAPP-HOOPER. Thank you so much for your question. I will just tack on to Dr. Erickson's remarks and note that I also do agree that the administration and the U.S. Government, by virtue of these freedom of navigation exercises, is doing its part toward objecting to the most objectionable parts of a potential ADIZ in the South China Sea.

We have also seen some recent statements by friends and allies in the region who suggested that they, too, would object to an air defense identification zone if China should declare one and attempt to enforce it in ways that are inimical to international law. That includes certainly Japan, it includes Australia.

So one other thing that the United States could do in advance of China's declaration of a South China Sea air defense identification zone is to prepare a multilateral groundwork to object to exercise if China is to try to implement an ADIZ in a way that runs counter to international law. That is, not to have the United States being the only country that flies through the airspace or transits the waters, but show that this is a problem for the region and for the rules-based system as a whole.

Mr. SWAINE. Just a couple of comments on this. I think the Chinese could very well announce an ADIZ for the South China Sea at some point. Their policy right now is that they have no intention of doing this at the time. They haven't committed that they will never do it. But they have never stated that an ADIZ is anything approaching territorial airspace. In fact, their objection to Japanese sorties that were sent up against Chinese aircraft in the ADIZ was that Japan treated it like territorial airspace.

The Chinese position on this I think would have to be measured by what exactly they are including in an ADIZ, because an ADIZ should have a relationship to a territorial airspace or territory. It is a buffer zone before you enter into that area.

Now, if the Chinese establish an ADIZ across the entire South China Sea, what is the territorial area that requires them to establish that ADIZ of that size? If they say it is everything in the Nine-

Dash Line, then they are essentially stating that the Nine-Dish Line is territorial airspace, territorial waters. And if they state that, they will be in complete violation of international law, and they will be taking an action which I think will be unanimously opposed, and they would have to take the consequences of that happening. Therefore, I think it is unlikely that they will do that, because they are not going to make that statement about the Nine-Dash Line area.

Now, they could make an ADIZ, but it all depends upon the conditions that they do it under. If they notify people in advance, if they state clearly exactly what the limits of it are and if that complies with law, and if they state clearly what the process is by which you can—by which they are going to enforce it, as they could attempt to do, then you can deal with that problem.

If they do it without informing anybody, they include the South China Sea as the whole, they make the implication that they have declared it as territorial airspace, then you have got a real problem. But it is not just the simple fact that they may declare an ADIZ. It really depends on what it is.

Mr. PERRY. Have any other countries continued to—I imagine all of the other countries in the neighborhood have continued to fly in the current ADIZ with impunity, so to speak? Or is it just the United States that continues to——

Mr. SWAINE. So you mean the East China Sea ADIZ?

Mr. PERRY. Yes.

Mr. SWAINE. Well, actually, airliners—the Chinese asked for notification for any sort of airliners it would cross through the air defense identification zone, even if they weren't going to enter into Chinese airspace. Airlines, including American airlines, do this.

Mr. PERRY. But is that kind of validating, like the quiet title to the airspace over time, by complying with what is——

Mr. SWAINE. Well, just one point on this. The Chinese are not unique in requiring or asking that foreign countries declare or notify them even when they are just transiting an ADIZ. They are not unique in that regard.

The United States believes an ADIZ should only be functioning if you are going to go and enter the airspace. Some other countries, including Japan, vis-à -vis Taiwan, require Taiwanese aircraft to notify the Japanese government when they are going through their Japanese ADIZ. So the Chinese are not unique in——

Mr. PERRY. But is the Japan situation unique, and China using that opportunity to say, ''Well, we want to do the same thing,'' without having any really relevant claim?

Mr. SWAINE. Well, what the Chinese did here—and I think it did relate to Japan—is they said Japan has an ADIZ. And have you ever seen a map of Japan with its ADIZ? It is very big. It extends out to about 130 kilometers from the Chinese coast. And the Chinese said, ''Okay. We have this dispute with the Japanese. We are trying to assert our administrative authority around the Senkaku Islands. We are going to have an ADIZ.''

The Chinese claimed that it didn't have to do with Japan, but that's baloney. It had to do with Japan.

Mr. PERRY. I will turn to Chairman Salmon.

Mr. SALMON. Yes. It looks like we have been buzzed for a vote, but I just have one quick question. There are no quick questions around here, right? Xi Jinping is going to be here after the August recess. September. September he is going to be here.

This is a really golden opportunity for us to raise some of these issues in a constructive way, I believe, with him. I know that obviously the President will be meeting with him, but several Members of Congress will have access to him as well. If you were in our spot, how would you approach it?

Mr. CRONIN. Mr. Chairman, thank you. It is a very important opportunity. Obviously, President Xi and President Obama both want a successful summit meeting. Both want to be seen as successful stewards of major power relations, and they have more on the agenda later in the year, especially at Paris over climate change where that is expected to be an area of cooperation between the two capitals and the two administrations.

We have a chance, therefore, to raise, in advance of the summit and at the summit, a serious discussion about the South China Sea. We need to get more specific about what we object to, what we are trying to prevent, including an ADIZ, about what our interests are and what our purposes are, and why other countries throughout the region have a right to be involved in upholding law, international law, the rule of law, and access to the global commons.

We ought to be coordinating with other countries in the region in advance as well to make sure that we don't, unfortunately, create the perception that we are just negotiating with China on what some are advocating should be a sphere of influence effectively for China. Just the opposite; we are trying to tamp down the tensions, so that all can continue to benefit.

We also need to be investing, though, in our long term. This is not going away this fall. This is going to be here for the rest of the century. We need to build up our regional expertise, our history, our geography, our cultural air, sea, law, expertise, through education, in our government. And this committee can help do that, sir, with its leadership.

Thank you, sir.

Mr. ERICKSON. Thank you, Mr. Chairman. It is a very important opportunity. Our engagement with China, indeed, is important, and in fact is based on many mutual interests. But we need to stand up for our own interests in this process. Part of that is getting the rhetoric right, the wording right.

And following what I call the Hippocratic Oath of International Relations: First, do no harm. In our messaging, don't use the term ''Thucydides trap.'' Don't use the term ''new type of great power relations'' or ''new type of major country relations'' or ''new model of relations,'' et cetera, et cetera, et cetera. Instead, China can say what it wants. We encourage freedom of speech. We want to promote this. But then we should advance our own formulations, our own positive ideas.

Under Bob Zoellick, the ''responsible stakeholder'' concept was one such very positive aspect. And, frankly, I think the current administration early on missed an opportunity to continue to put out its own formulation, and instead ''new type great power relations'' came in to fill the void. So the substance behind the words matters, but so, too, do the words.

Thank you.

Ms. RAPP-HOOPER. Mr. Chairman, I think that in this very important summit the United States should take the opportunity to communicate not only its interests in broad abstractions but, as my colleagues have mentioned, what those actions are that China may take that may be inimical to those interests.

So, again, we often have a tendency to speak in terms such as freedom of navigation, freedom of overflight, but it is important to highlight that the reason that this P–8 video that was released by CNN was so worrisome was because it suggested that freedom of navigation and freedom of overflight could already be in jeopardy. That is, because a U.S. aircraft was warned away from an artificial island, told that it was approaching a military zone.

So being specific about the types of warnings, the types of actions that would cause the greatest concern in the United States is an absolute must. Additionally, I think this is a really important opportunity to lay down some criteria for what constitutes militarization of an island versus what constitutes civilian use of an island.

And this is not just applicable to China, but, rather, to all of the claimants who may have facilities and outposts in the Spratly Islands. This is because if we are ambiguous, if we don't clarify this criteria, there is the possibility that China will continue to advance its militarization of the islands very quickly, or that it may install dual use equipment that may be destabilizing, that may take other claimants by surprise, and that this may proceed in fits and starts in ways that can be deeply destabilizing to things such as Code of Conduct negotiations.

So taking this opportunity to clarify intentions on both sides, to specify intentions on both sides, I think is absolutely the order of the day.

Thank you very much.

Mr. SWAINE. I agree with my colleagues about the importance of this issue, and I think it should definitely be raised during the Xi Jinping visit to the United States. It is really that significant an issue. This could become a serious source of a deterioration in this relationship over these rocks and islands in the South China Sea, of a relationship that is gigantic, where these two powers are really joined at the hip in many ways.

So the two countries have to work to avoid that. I don't think it is going to happen if you have a staged discussion of this issue between two sides with generic talking points. You will just get the same exchange of information that we have had before.

I think Obama needs to sit down with Xi Jinping, with a small number of staff, and talk seriously about this issue, talk about what U.S. concerns are, talk about what the United States would see as unacceptable in certain ways, and then talk about ways in which the two sides can reassure each other that these things are not going to happen. And the Chinese can express their views as well.

When Kerry was in Beijing not long ago, Xi Jinping apparently told him, ''We have no desire or intention to do things that will provoke or upset the United States.'' Well, they should follow up on that and take him up on this and try to engage him directly on this.

One last point. I really disagree fundamentally with my friend Andrew's view about the new type of great power relations. I don't think there is any problem with that concept. I think it in fact captures what China and the United States should be doing. We don't have to accept the Chinese definition of what that means. Just because the Chinese raised it doesn't mean for some reason we shouldn't be supporting it.

We want to see a region evolve here where in fact there is a clear avoidance of the kind of power rivalries that you will get from a rising power that is in some ways a non-status quo power in the Western Pacific, and a dominant power, the United States.

In my view, the level of American predominance that we have enjoyed for 70 years in the Western Pacific is and will erode. We will lose our position, relatively speaking, to the Chinese. Yes, we have to keep up deterrence capabilities. Yes, we have to defend our most vital interests and will. But at the same time, our image and our capability as the predominant maritime power in the Western Pacific, in my view, is going to be gone.

The Chinese will have capabilities that will call into question that surety of that American position. The question is: What do we do about that? And, to my mind, the strategy should be thinking about how you can transition to a stable balance of power in the Western Pacific.

Thank you.

Mr. PERRY. The acting chair thanks the panelists. Thank you very much for the great discussion. It was kind of great not to have so many people here, so Matt and I could ask all the questions. But we appreciate your interest and your involvement, and we look forward to working with you in the future as well as the other members. And at this time, this hearing is adjourned.

[Whereupon, at 3:53 p.m., the subcommittee was adjourned.]

APPENDIX

MATERIAL SUBMITTED FOR THE RECORD

SUBCOMMITTEE HEARING NOTICE
COMMITTEE ON FOREIGN AFFAIRS
U.S. HOUSE OF REPRESENTATIVES
WASHINGTON, DC 20515-6128

Subcommittee on Asia and the Pacific
Matt Salmon (R-AZ), Chairman

July 23, 2015

TO: MEMBERS OF THE COMMITTEE ON FOREIGN AFFAIRS

You are respectfully requested to attend an OPEN hearing of the Committee on Foreign Affairs, to be held by the Subcommittee on Asia and the Pacific in Room 2172 of the Rayburn House Office Building (and available live on the Committee website at http://www.ForeignAffairs.house.gov):

DATE: Thursday, July 23, 2015

TIME: 2:00 p.m.

SUBJECT: America's Security Role in the South China Sea

WITNESSES: Patrick M. Cronin, Ph.D.
Senior Advisor and Senior Director
Asia-Pacific Security Program
Center for a New American Security

Andrew S. Erickson, Ph.D.
Associate Professor
China Maritime Studies Institute
U.S. Naval War College

Mira Rapp Hooper, Ph.D.
Fellow, Asia Program
Director, Asia Maritime Transparency Initiative
Center for Strategic & International Studies

Michael D. Swaine, Ph.D.
Senior Associate
Asia Program
Carnegie Endowment for International Peace

By Direction of the Chairman

The Committee on Foreign Affairs seeks to make its facilities accessible to persons with disabilities. If you are in need of special accommodations, please call 202/225-5021 at least four business days in advance of the event, whenever practicable. Questions with regard to special accommodations in general (including availability of Committee materials in alternative formats and assistive listening devices) may be directed to the Committee.

COMMITTEE ON FOREIGN AFFAIRS

MINUTES OF SUBCOMMITTEE ON _____ *Asia and the Pacific* _____ HEARING

Day___ *Thursday*___ Date_____ *7/23/15*_____ Room_____ *2172*_____

Starting Time _____ *2:29* _____ Ending Time _____ *3:53* _____

Recesses [_____] (____to ____) (____to ____) (____to ____) (____to ____) (____to ____) (____to ____)

Presiding Member(s)

Perry

Check all of the following that apply:

Open Session ☑   Electronically Recorded (taped) ☐
Executive (closed) Session ☐   Stenographic Record ☐
Televised ☐

TITLE OF HEARING:

America's Security Role in the South China Sea

SUBCOMMITTEE MEMBERS PRESENT:

DesJarlais, Brooks, Salmon
Sherman, Bera, Meng

NON-SUBCOMMITTEE MEMBERS PRESENT: *(Mark with an * if they are not members of full committee.)*

HEARING WITNESSES: Same as meeting notice attached? Yes ☑ No ☐
(If "no", please list below and include title, agency, department, or organization.)

STATEMENTS FOR THE RECORD: *(List any statements submitted for the record.)*

Connolly

TIME SCHEDULED TO RECONVENE _____
or
TIME ADJOURNED _____ *3:53* _____

_____
Subcommittee Staff Director

68

MATERIAL SUBMITTED FOR THE RECORD BY THE HONORABLE MATT SALMON, A REPRESENTATIVE IN CONGRESS FROM THE STATE OF ARIZONA, AND CHAIRMAN, SUBCOMMITTEE ON ASIA AND THE PACIFIC

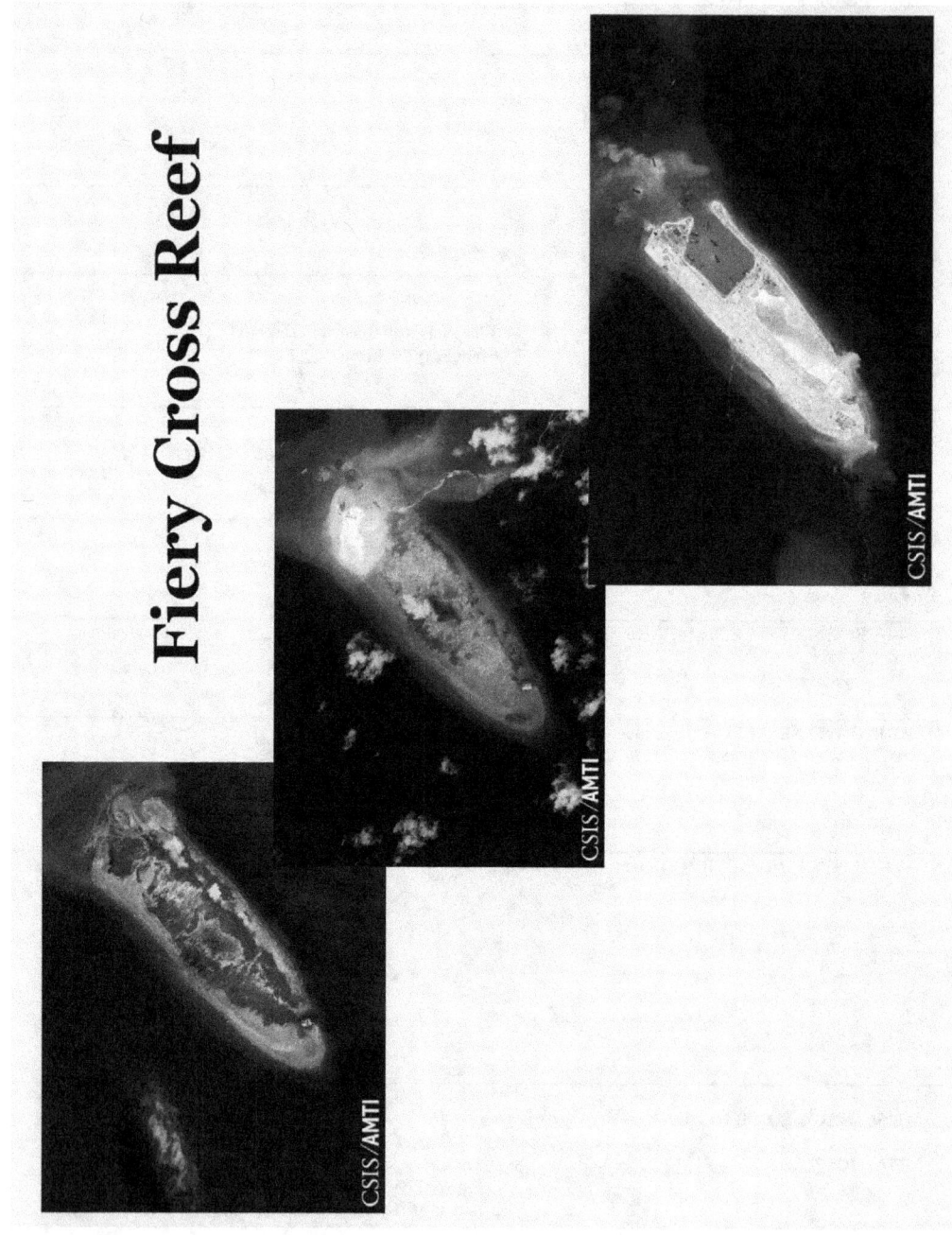

Fiery Cross Reef

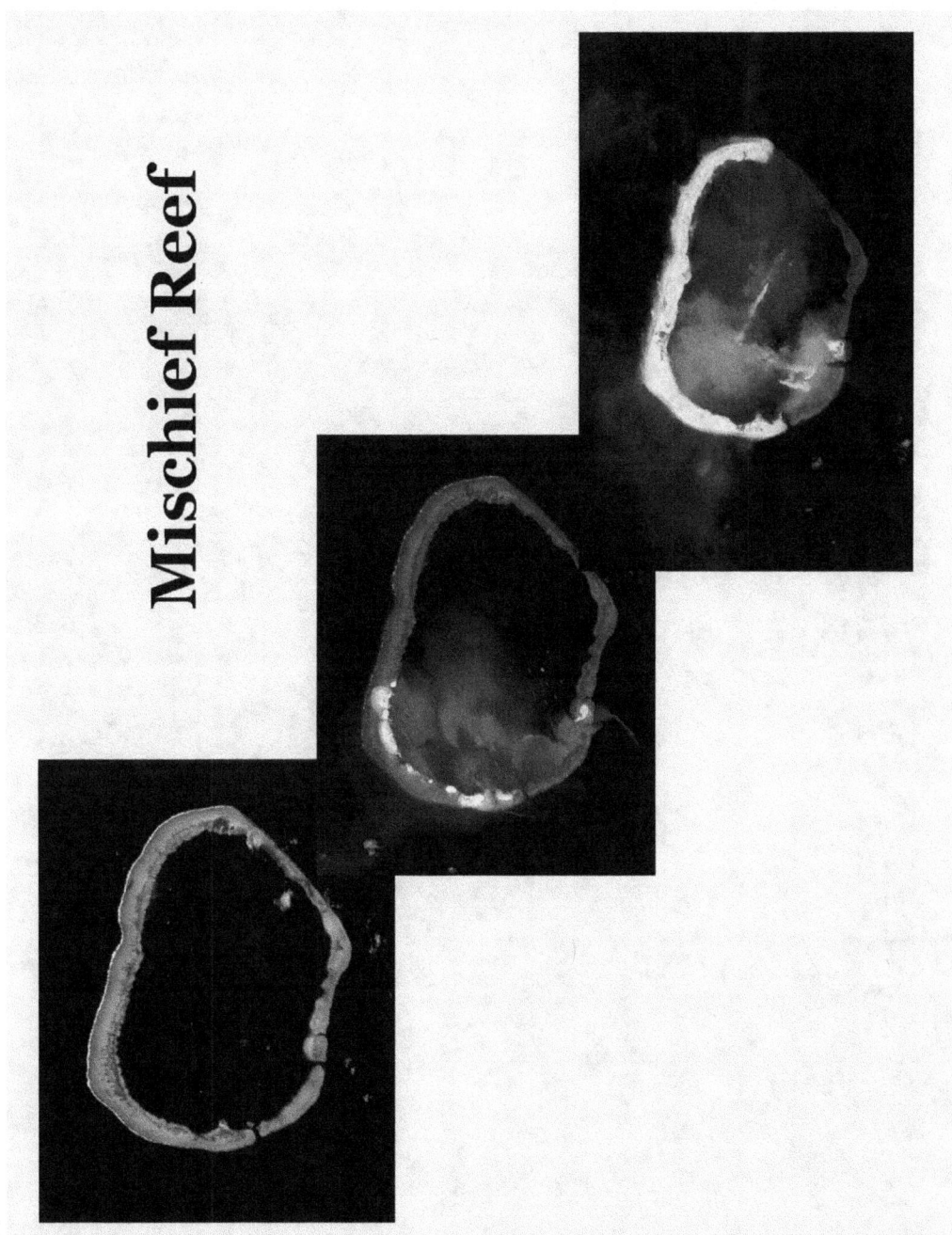

China's Nine-Dash Line

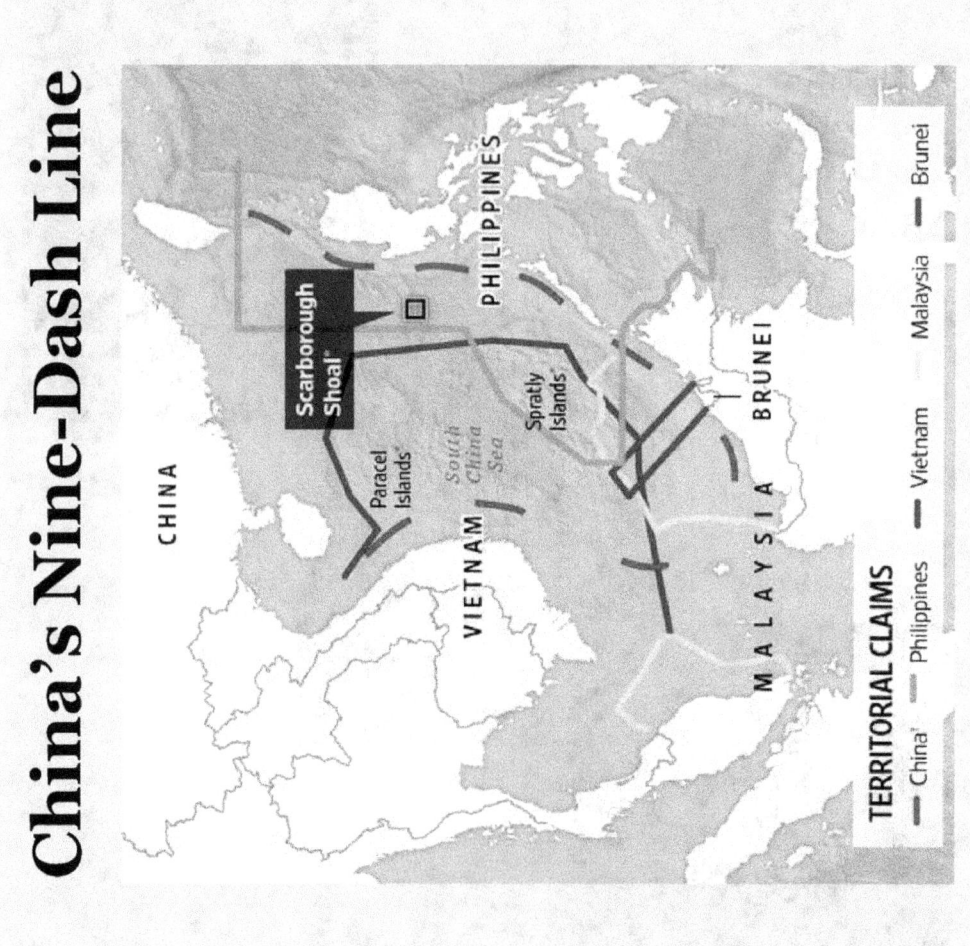

Statement for the Record
Submitted by Mr. Connolly of Virginia

Last week, this Subcommittee examined U.S. military alliances and security partnerships in the Asia-Pacific. Several witnesses testified on the importance of these relationships as the "cornerstones" of U.S. foreign and security policy in the Asia-Pacific. The U.S. and our Asia-Pacific partners collaborate on regional security, within multilateral institutions, through trade, and on a host of other activities that depend on trust and mutual interest.

China's aggression in the South China Sea threatens the regional order based on cooperation and international law promoted by the U.S. and our partners. Failure to diffuse or resolve the South China Sea disputes in a manner consistent with international law, such as the United Nations Convention on the Law of the Sea (UNCLOS), and the security interests of our partners would erode U.S. credibility in the region and potentially redefine the treatment of the world's oceans as an international commons.

Among the claimants to disputed areas of the South China Sea are China, Taiwan, Japan, Vietnam, the Philippines, Brunei, and Malaysia. The U.S. has mutual defense relationships with Japan and the Philippines and a longstanding and statutory defense partnership with Taiwan. While U.S. maritime assistance packages to the countries of the Asia-Pacific are an order of magnitude smaller than China's maritime modernization and construction program, Congress did authorize the transfer of four Perry-class guided missile frigates to Taiwan in 2014 – an effort I was glad to help lead as a co-chair of the Congressional Taiwan Caucus.

Considering both the risk for confrontation that is emerging in the South China Sea and our standing security commitments, it is difficult to divorce U.S. national security interests from the peaceful resolution of territorial claims and navigation rights in the South China Sea.

It was then-Secretary of State Hillary Clinton who announced at the 2010 ASEAN Regional Forum that the United States has a "national interest in freedom of navigation, open access to Asia's maritime commons, and respect for international law in the South China Sea." The U.S. has also condemned the use of coercion, threat, or the use of force to assert territorial claims in the South China Sea.

However, it is not immediately clear that U.S. policy has accomplished much beyond reassuring China's neighbors that the U.S. does not condone China's aggressive actions. China has carried out reclamation activities that have created more than 2,000 acres of new territory on seven land masses in the Spratly Islands. This includes the construction of a 10,000-foot runway on one of the once-tiny outcroppings. Despite U.S. support for the 1992 ASEAN Declaration on the South China Sea, the 2002 ASEAN-China Declaration on the Conduct of Parties in the South China Sea, and the ASEAN Six-Point Principles on the South China Sea, most experts agree that a consensus on a comprehensive Code of Conduct is not in the region's immediate future.

The U.S. does not dispute China's right to regulate economic activity within its Exclusive Economic Zone (EEZ), defined by waters within 200 nautical miles of legitimate land features. However, the U.S. has consistently challenged China's authority to restrict freedom of navigation for military assets within its

EEZ. The U.S. has thus far asserted its navigation and flyover rights in China's EEZ by conducting surveillance and military activities despite protests from China. Last week, Admiral Scott Swift, commander of the U.S. Pacific Fleet, participated in a surveillance flight in the South China Sea that was quickly condemned by Chinese authorities.

Admiral Scott's activity is consistent with principles endorsed by the House of Representatives. In the 113th Congress, this Subcommittee reported out House Resolution 714 – legislation sponsored by our esteemed former colleague Rep. Eni Faleomavaega. The measure affirmed support for a peaceful resolution of maritime disputes in the South China Sea, but also encouraged continued U.S. operations consistent with the principle of freedom of navigation in international waters and airspace. The measure was agreed to without objection by the full House in December 2014.

However, a continuation of the status quo may no longer be sufficient for U.S. policy decisions in the South China Sea. China has ramped up shipbuilding to support a massive build up of Coast Guard ocean-going patrol ships and small Navy assets. A 2015 Department of Defense assessment concluded that, "during periods of tension in the South China Sea, China uses the quantity and advanced capabilities of its CCG assets to overwhelm and deter South China Sea claimant nations with the goal of eventually compelling regional acceptance of China's sovereignty claims."

Demonstrations of overwhelming force do not constitute a productive trajectory for South China Sea maritime disputes. The relationship with China in the South China Sea must be managed. I look forward to hearing from our witness on how the U.S. can deescalate the situation in the South China Sea in a manner that respects the complexity and historical nature of this conflict. The modern disputes in the South China Sea may be only decades-old tensions, but the countries reach back millennia to legitimize their claims. Claimants must be able to differentiate between national interest and national pride, and China must demonstrate that it will be a willing participant in a rules-based international order where rules are not rewritten to serve its narrow interests.